for the love of food

for the love
of food

recipes and stories from
the chefs of the iacp

international association of culinary professionals

for the love **of food**

recipes and stories from
the chefs of the iacp

Published by The International Association of Culinary Professionals

Executive Editor: Sarah R. Labensky, CCP
Executive Director: Daniel D. Maye

This cookbook is a collection of favorite recipes,
which are not necessarily original recipes.

Library of Congress Control Number: 2005920982
ISBN: 0-9764517-0-0

Edited, designed, manufactured, and marketed by
Favorite Recipes® Press
an imprint of

FRP

The proud sponsor of *For the Love of Food*

P.O. Box 305142
Nashville, Tennessee 37230
800-358-0560

Editorial Director: Mary Cummings   Art Director: Steve Newman
Project Editor: Jane Hinshaw   Book Design: David Malone
Project Manager: Debbie Van Mol   Production Designer: Travis Rader
Assistant Editor: Ashley Bienvenu

Senior Publishing Consultant: Bob Johnson
Marketing Director: Mary Margaret Andrews

Pages 168 through 171 are an extension of the copyright page.

Printed in the United States of America
First printing: 2005
10,000 copies

foreword

Every practicing chef has a different story, a different recipe, and his or her own unique perspective on food and dining. In *For the Love of Food*, you are invited to share the personal experiences and coveted recipes of thirty-four of the world's greatest cooks. This delightful collection of stories and recipes offers the reader an opportunity to peek into the lives of these professional cooks, as well as to prepare proven signature dishes from chef members of the International Association of Culinary Professionals.

The common denominator in this work is the love for food and the professional integrity of the contributors. All of the work appearing in this book comes from IACP members: the food styling, the photography, the writing, and, of course, the recipes. The photography itself is award worthy and makes the book a wonderful coffee table addition.

You will not find only one favorite recipe in this collection. All are noteworthy, and all capture the spirit and enthusiasm of the cooking professionals who contributed them. The title, *For the Love of Food*, couldn't be more appropriate. It is easy to recognize the commitment these chefs have to their craft, in addition to total devotion to the ingredients utilized in the recipes. There are recipes for every mood and occasion, and techniques are explained to help you re-create these favorites.

You'll find yourself caught up in these pages getting to know the chefs and familiarizing yourself with their wonderful recipes. So please enjoy this culinary masterpiece…for the love of food!

Shirley Corriher, CCP   Christian "Kit" Kiefer, CEC, CCE

table of **contents**

samarnold &
hollykinney

Time-Life Books has referred to Sam Arnold as a "food historian, chef de cuisine, journalist, world traveler, restaurateur, raconteur . . . Sam Arnold is a gold mine of information."

Sam Arnold is the founder and co-owner of The Fort Restaurant, a castle-like replica of the 1834 Bent's Fort, Colorado's first fur-trading post, nestled against scenic red rocks near Morrison, Colorado. Holly Arnold Kinney and her brother, Keith, were raised in the restaurant. In 2001, Kinney became her father's business partner and co-owner of the landmark restaurant. Her most recent endeavor was launching the Web-based Fort Trading Company in 2003 to market and sell The Fort's world-renowned buffalo, elk, and quail around the country.

Sam is recognized nationally as an authority on foods of the Southwest and early West and has written several books on the subject, including *Eating Up the Santa Fe Trail*, illustrated by his late wife, Carrie. It includes research of diaries and journals kept by early-nineteenth-century settlers, trappers, and traders. His most recent cookbook is *The Fort Cookbook: New Foods of the Old West from the Famous Denver Restaurant*. Arnold has also hosted and produced regional and national television shows.

Arnold was named Denver's Own Chile Guru by *Bon Appétit* magazine and Queso Grande of the Colorado Chapter of International Connoisseurs of Green and Red Chile. In 1997, Arnold was honored to host President Clinton's state dinner during the World Leaders Summit of the Eight Conference, held in Denver. In May 2004, Arnold was presented with an honorary Doctor of Business Administration in Food Service Management from Johnson and Wales University, recognizing his "pioneering spirit of the Old West" and his "entrepreneurial drive and resolve to achieve his aspirations."

In 1981, Kinney founded Arnold Media Services, a public relations firm specializing in the specialty food products and restaurant industry. It has provided public relations, marketing, advertising, and promotion services for local, national, and international clientele. In 2002, Arnold Media Services became the in-house public relations, advertising, and graphic design agency for The Fort Restaurant.

Photographer
ricksouders

Food Stylist
steviebass

*Arnold's zest for living stems
from the roasted whole chile of life.*

negrita

recipesrecipes

Jalapeños Stuffed with Peanut Butter

Negrita

Teriyaki Quail Game Plate

**samarnold
& hollykinney 9**

jalapeños
stuffed with peanut butter

Lucy Delgado, well known in the 1960s as a traditionalist New Mexican cook, taught me to stuff peanut butter into peppers. "If I show you how to make them, you have to promise to try them." Peanut butter-stuffed jalapeños! I vowed I would taste them even though they sounded stranger than a five-legged buffalo. She instructed me to "pop the entire pepper into your mouth so you're not left with a mouthful of hot jalapeño and too little peanut butter." I gamely took the little morsel by the stem, and in it went. Miracle! Delicious! I made them for my own parties until they became so popular that I put them on the menu. When NBC's Today Show came to Denver, Bryant Gumbel ate eight of them in a row, although Jane Pauley would have none of it.

A fun variation is to mix Major Grey's chutney with the peanut butter. It gives a nice fruity sweetness that also buffers the burn.

serves **10**

1 (12-ounce) can pickled jalapeño peppers
1 1/2 cups smooth or chunky peanut butter

Slice the pickled jalapeños into halves lengthwise, cutting not quite all the way through and leaving the 2 halves attached at the stem end. Using a knife or spoon, remove the seeds and ribs under running water. Pack the halves with the peanut butter and press together. Arrange on a serving plate. Be sure to warn guests to put everything but the stem in their mouths before chewing in order to get 70 percent peanut butter and 30 percent jalapeño. A nibbler squeezes out the peanut butter, changing the percentages and making it very hot indeed.

negrita

The negrita, or "little black one," originated in the Vera Cruz region of Mexico. While it bears a resemblance to chocolate mousse, its texture is very different—firmer, like a slightly soft chocolate bar. Unlike many highly concentrated chocolate desserts, of which a few bites are enough, this one begs for the dish to be scraped (or licked) clean. A spoonful on the tip of the tongue followed by hot coffee is luscious. This recipe can be halved.

serves **10**

1 1/4 pounds Ghirardelli sweet dark chocolate
6 eggs
1 tablespoon vanilla extract
1/4 cup rum
1/2 pint heavy cream, whipped, for topping

Place the chocolate in a double boiler over simmering water; do not let the water touch the bottom of the bowl holding the chocolate. Cook until half-melted, stirring occasionally. Remove from the heat and leave it over the warm water to finish melting and to keep it warm. It is important not to let the chocolate cool too much before blending with the other ingredients, or it will become grainy. If you think it has become too cool by the time you're ready to use it, place on the heat to warm it slightly.

Separate the eggs. Beat the egg whites until stiff in a clean dry bowl. Beat the egg yolks until they are pale yellow in a separate bowl.

Add the chocolate, vanilla and rum to the egg yolks carefully, then fold in the beaten egg whites, mixing until thoroughly blended. Ladle into 2 1/2-ounce ramekins or wine glasses and chill. Serve topped with whipped cream.

teriyaki **quail game plate**

The West was built in good part by Chinese and Japanese immigrants who supplied both hands and brains to build railroads and cities, ranches and farms. Also, some of the first trappers who had been brought to our northwest coast by John Jacob Astor were Hawaiians. It is not surprising, therefore, that teriyaki came to the West early on.

In The Fort's most popular entrée, The Game Plate, teriyaki quail is accompanied by a lightly seasoned buffalo filet and elk medallion grilled over an open flame to rare or medium-rare.

serves **8**

1 cup soy sauce
$1/2$ cup rice wine or dry sherry
$1/4$ cup sugar
2 tablespoons minced fresh ginger
3 cloves garlic, minced
2 whole star anise
$1/4$ cup finely chopped orange peel
1 cup orange juice
1 cup water
8 ($2^{1}/2$- to $3^{1}/2$-ounce) partially deboned quail
4 orange slices, for garnish

Combine the soy sauce, rice wine, sugar, ginger, garlic, star anise, orange peel, orange juice and water in a saucepan for the marinade. Bring to a boil over high heat. Lower the heat and simmer for 5 minutes. Let cool.

Place the quail in a single layer in a pan and pour the marinade over the quail. Marinate for 2 to 4 hours. Beware of leaving the birds in for more than 8 hours because they will become unpalatably salty.

Heat the grill to medium or preheat the broiler when ready to cook the quail. Grill or broil the quail for 3 to 4 minutes on each side. Garnish with a twisted orange slice.

Serve with a buffalo tenderloin and elk medallion. We recommend only fresh cuts of meat if available. Have a hot grill for cooking, season the buffalo and elk with a char crust, and cook to medium-rare or medium for the best flavor.

lidia**bastianich**

Lidia Bastianich, the warm hostess of her own cooking show and mistress of Italian-American cooking, is also a cookbook author and highly successful restaurateur with two of Manhattan's most notable restaurants, Felidia and Becco.

In 1998, she opened Lidia's Kansas City with her son, Joseph, and David Wagner. She opened Lidia's Pittsburgh in 2001. In addition, she has launched a line of prepared pasta sauces. She has authored several highly acclaimed books, including *La Cucina di Lidia*, *Lidia's Italian Table*, and *Lidia's Italian-American Kitchen*, which is also the name of her fifty-two-part television series. She is writing a new cookbook with her daughter, Tanya, an art historian, exploring the themes of Italian art and food. In 1996, she and Tanya launched a company that conducts food, wine, and cultural tours of Italy. In 1999, she was named Best Chef in New York by the James Beard Foundation.

Lidia's claim to knowledge of Italian cooking has deep roots, for she grew up in Istria, a coastal region of Italy that is now part of Croatia. There, she acquired her love of Italian cooking, where, she says, every meal is a celebration of life, love, and history. Her advice for cooks eager to replicate authentic Italian cuisine is to keep it simple: Cook with the highest quality ingredients, but don't overwhelm the palate with too many ingredients. And, above all, relax and enjoy the sharing of love, tradition, and family.

My life ever since I can remember revolved around food. When I was a child, three generations gathered in the family compound or courtyard and performed the growing, caring for, milling, drying, preserving, and cooking of food for a small inn my grandmother ran. As a young girl in convent school, I happily helped in the kitchen to supplement my tuition. Beginning as a new immigrant to America at fourteen, I worked part-time in bakeries and restaurants to help the family. I opened my first restaurant with my husband when I was twenty-four—a thirty-seven-seat Italian restaurant. Could all of this be pure destiny or coincidence? I do not think so. After thirty-four years, five restaurants, four cookbooks, a National Public Television cooking program, and with both children, Tanya and Joseph, joining me in the business, I am still as excited and as passionate about food as I was. It must be love.

Photographer
billschilling

Food Stylist
debbiewahl

I love all food; I just happen to be Italian, and what a blessing that is!

braised lamb shanks in squazet

recipesrecipes

Braised Lamb Shanks in Squazet

Roasted Pears and Grapes

Tomato and Bread Soup

Roasted Beet Salad with Figs and Goat Cheese

lidia**bastianich** 13

braised lamb shanks in squazet

serves **6**

1/2 cup dried porcini
   mushrooms

2 cups hot water

2 oranges

4 fresh or dried bay leaves

2 sprigs fresh rosemary

4 whole cloves

6 (1-pound) lamb shanks

salt and freshly ground
   black pepper to taste

1/4 cup extra-virgin olive oil

2 cups minced onions

1/4 cup minced pancetta
   or bacon

1 cup dry red wine,
   such as Barolo

1/4 cup tomato paste

6 cups chicken stock or
   low-sodium canned
   chicken broth

The best shanks for this recipe are foreshanks, preferably cut so as to include a little of the leg above the knee joint. Because of their size and shape, they are a little more difficult to work with, and you probably have to brown them in two or three batches. If you cannot find these larger shanks, use six of the easier-to-find shanks cut below the knee.

Soak the porcini in the hot water in a bowl until softened, about 20 minutes. Strain the porcini and soaking liquid through a coffee filter or a sieve lined with a double thickness of cheesecloth. Rinse the mushrooms and pick off any tough bits. Reserve the mushrooms and soaking liquid separately.

Remove the zest, orange portion only, from the oranges in long strips with a vegetable peeler. Squeeze the juice from the oranges and reserve the juice and zest. Tie the bay leaves, rosemary and cloves securely in a 4-inch-square piece of cheesecloth.

Season the lamb shanks generously with salt and pepper. Heat the olive oil in a wide heavy saucepan large enough to hold the shanks. Add the onions and pancetta to the saucepan and season them lightly with salt and pepper. Sauté until golden brown, about 8 minutes. Remove with a slotted spoon, leaving as much oil in the saucepan as possible. Add as many of the lamb shanks as will fit in a single layer. Sauté, turning the shanks occasionally, until all the liquid has evaporated and the lamb begins to brown, about 15 minutes. Remove the lamb shanks and repeat with the remaining shanks if necessary.

Return the onion mixture to the saucepan. Add the porcini, cheesecloth bundle of herbs, orange zest and orange juice. Cook for 5 minutes. Add the wine and cook, stirring occasionally, until the wine has almost completely evaporated, about 10 minutes. Stir in the tomato paste and season lightly with salt and pepper. Add the reserved mushroom soaking liquid and enough of the chicken stock to cover the shanks.

Bring to a boil and reduce the heat to moderately low. Simmer, partially covered, until the lamb is tender and the sauce is slightly thickened, about 1 1/2 hours, turning the shanks in the sauce occasionally.

If serving the shanks with spaetzle, prepare the spaetzle batter when the lamb begins to simmer. Bring the water to a boil and cook the spaetzle about 10 minutes before the lamb is finished cooking.

Remove the lamb shanks to a serving platter. Strain the sauce into a wide skillet and bring to a boil over high heat. Boil until the sauce is thickened enough to lightly coat a spoon. Spoon over and around the shanks. If serving with the spaetzle, leave about 1/2 cup of the sauce in the skillet. Remove the spaetzle from the cooking water with a slotted spoon and add to the sauce in the skillet. Cook until the sauce is reduced enough to coat the spaetzle.

roasted pears and grapes

serves **6**

2 cups seedless red grapes
1 cup sugar
juice of 2 lemons
2/3 cup moscato
1/2 vanilla bean, split lengthwise
2 tablespoons apricot jam
3 firm ripe Bosc pears

Preheat the oven to 375 degrees. Place the grapes in a 7×11-inch baking dish. Combine the sugar, lemon juice, moscato, vanilla bean and apricot jam in a bowl and stir to mix well. Pour over the grapes. Cut the pears into halves lengthwise through the cores and remove the cores and seeds. Nestle the pear halves cut side up in the grapes.

Bake until the pears are tender and the liquid around the grapes is thick and syrupy, about 50 minutes. Remove the pears and let stand for about 10 minutes. Spoon some of the grapes into serving compotes and add a pear half to each compote. Top with the remaining grapes and cooking syrup.

tomato and bread soup

The ripeness and flavor of the tomatoes is imperative for this dish. Therefore, make the soup when the tomatoes are abundant and ripe and at their best—in late summer. This "zuppa" is delicious warm or served at room temperature on a hot summer day.

serves 8

5 (^{1}/2-inch) slices Italian bread, crusts removed
3 tablespoons extra-virgin olive oil, plus additional for serving
^{1}/2 cup finely diced onion
6 garlic cloves, peeled and crushed
2 pounds ripe plum tomatoes, peeled, seeded and juice reserved, or 1 undrained (35-ounce) can
      Italian plum tomatoes, preferably San Marzano, seeded and cut into ^{1}/2-inch pieces
4 cups chicken stock
salt and freshly ground black pepper to taste
10 fresh basil leaves

Preheat the oven to 375 degrees. Arrange the bread slices on a baking sheet and toast until light golden brown, about 10 minutes. Remove and set aside.

Heat 3 tablespoons olive oil in a deep heavy 4- to 5-quart saucepan over medium heat. Add the onion and sauté, stirring, until wilted, about 3 minutes. Add the garlic and sauté until golden brown, about 6 minutes.

Add the tomatoes and their juices to the saucepan. Bring to a boil, stirring occasionally. Add the toasted bread and chicken stock and return to a boil. Season with salt and pepper.

Add the basil leaves and reduce the heat to a simmer. Simmer, uncovered, whisking occasionally to break up the bread, until the mixture is thick and smooth, about 40 minutes.

Remove the garlic and basil leaves if desired. Strain the soup through a fine sieve, pressing the solids through with a ladle. You may first process the soup with a food mill fitted with a fine disk if desired. Correct the seasonings. Serve in warm bowls and drizzle with additional extra-virgin olive oil.

roasted beet salad
with figs and goat cheese

This version of a classic salad is made with figs. It can also be made with one cup matchstick-cut Granny Smith apple or four peeled and sliced ripe peaches.

serves 8

1 pound small yellow beets
1 pound small red beets
16 ripe Black Mission figs, cut into halves
1/4 cup extra-virgin olive oil
2 tablespoons red wine vinegar
1 tablespoon balsamic vinegar
salt and pepper to taste
1 (6-ounce) block slightly aged goat cheese, crumbled

Preheat the oven to 400 degrees. Clean the beets, discarding the root tips. Cut off and blanch the stems and leaves. Pierce the beets all over with a fork and place in a roasting pan. Roast until tender when pierced with a paring knife, 45 minutes to 1 1/2 hours, depending on the beets. Let the beets stand until cool enough to handle, then peel. Cut each beet into 6 or 8 slices.

Cut the blanched beet stems into 1-inch pieces. Combine the beets, figs and blanched leaves and stems in a bowl. Whisk the olive oil, red wine vinegar and balsamic vinegar together in a bowl. Add to the beet mixture and season with salt and pepper; toss to coat well. Spoon onto serving plates and drizzle with the dressing. Sprinkle with the goat cheese and serve.

As children in Italy, we made bread dolls out of the pinza dough used to make bread at Easter. We used colored hard-boiled eggs for heads and braided dough for blankets. My grandmother Rosa would take the bread dolls to church to be blessed along with the rest of the pinza loaves. I carried mine around like a baby for a few days before giving in to hunger and eating it from the toes up.

rick**bayless**

Rick Bayless was born into an Oklahoma City family of restaurateurs specializing in the local barbecue. He broadened his horizons to include regional Mexican cooking as an undergraduate student of Spanish and Latin American culture.

After hosting the twenty-six-part PBS television series *Cooking Mexican* in 1978 and 1979, Rick dedicated over six years to culinary research in Mexico, culminating in 1987 with the publication of his now-classic *Authentic Mexican: Regional Cooking from the Heart of Mexico*. Released in 1996, *Rick Bayless's Mexican Kitchen: Capturing the Vibrant Flavors of a World-Class Cuisine* was chosen Best Cookbook of the Year by the IACP/Julia Child Cookbook Awards and the *Chicago Tribune*. In 1999, Rick and his wife Deann, along with Jean Marie Brownson, released *Salsas That Cook*.

In 1987, the Baylesses opened the colorful, vivacious Frontera Grill in Chicago, specializing in contemporary regional Mexican cooking. In 1989 came the earthy, elegant Topolobampo, one of America's only fine-dining Mexican restaurants. Both restaurants have received numerous awards. In 1995, Bayless and partners started the extremely successful Frontera Foods line of prepared food products.

Rick Bayless was chosen Best New Chef of 1988 by *Food and Wine* magazine; in 1991, the James Beard Foundation voted him Best American Chef: Midwest; and in 1995, he won both the Beard Foundation's National Chef of the Year award and the International Association of Culinary Professionals' Chef of the Year award. Rick has been inducted into the prestigious Who's Who of American Food and Drink, and in 1998 was chosen as the Beard Foundation's Humanitarian of the Year. In the summer of 2000, Rick released his new public television series, *Mexico One Plate at a Time*, a twenty-six-part series with a companion book.

He supports environmentally sound agricultural practices and hunger advocacy organizations. Rick works as a restaurant consultant, teaches authentic Mexican cooking throughout the United States, is a visiting staff member at the Culinary Institute of America, and leads cooking and cultural tours to Mexico.

Photographer
eric**futran**

Food Stylist
irene**bertolucci**

...the greatest contribution to the Mexican table imaginable

tortilla soup

recipesrecipes

Tortilla Soup with Pasilla Chile, Fresh Cheese and Avocado

Roasted Poblano Guacamole with Garlic and Parsley

Quick-Fried Shrimp with Sweet Toasty Garlic

Tequila-Flamed Mangoes

rick**bayless** 19

tortilla soup
with pasilla chile, fresh cheese and avocado

serves
6 as a first course,
4 as a light main dish

6 corn tortillas

vegetable oil for frying

*4 garlic cloves, peeled and
left whole*

1 small white onion, sliced

*2 dried pasilla chiles, or
1 dried ancho chile,
stemmed, seeded and torn
into several flat pieces*

*1 (15-ounce) can good-quality
whole tomatoes in juice,
drained, or 12 ounces
(2 medium-small round)
ripe tomatoes, cored and
coarsely chopped*

6 cups good chicken broth

*1 large sprig fresh epazote
(optional)*

1/2 teaspoon salt, or to taste

*6 ounces Mexican queso
fresco or other crumbly fresh
cheese, such as pressed
salted farmer's cheese or
feta, cut into 1/2-inch cubes,
or 1 1/2 cups (6 ounces)
shredded Mexican melting
cheese (Chihuahua, quesillo
or asadero), Monterey Jack
or brick or mild Cheddar*

*1 large ripe avocado,
peeled, pitted and cut into
1/2-inch cubes*

1 large lime, cut into wedges

Yesterday's bread, first crisped to give new life, then set adrift in nourishing broth, softening as it soaks in the goodness—it's a recipe for soup of lasting memory. And tortilla soup is all of that. Like French onion soup, the world's most famous bread-topped potage, the Mexican "bread soup" is classic and timeless. The daily bread of Mexico, the corn tortilla, is a bread so immediate and fresh that (just like real French bread) it goes stale quickly. That reality has given rise to myriad creative uses for "leftovers," from enchiladas to casseroles to dumplings. And in soup, the stale tortillas find a perfect Mexican expression.

Cut the tortillas into halves, then into 1/4-inch strips. Heat 1/2 inch oil to 350 degrees in a 4-quart saucepan over medium heat. (Using a thermometer is most accurate, but there are other reliable clues: the oil releases that "hot oil" aroma and its surface begins shimmering. Without a thermometer, test the edge of a tortilla strip to ensure that it sizzles vigorously. Remember, smoking oil is dangerously overheated and will give the tortilla strips a bad taste.) Add half the tortilla strips. Fry, stirring nearly constantly, until they are golden brown and crispy. Scoop them out with a slotted spoon and drain on paper towels. Repeat with the remaining tortillas.

Pour off all but a thin coating of the hot oil and return the saucepan to the heat. Add the garlic and onion to the oil and cook, stirring regularly, until golden brown, about 7 minutes. Use a slotted spoon to scoop out the garlic and onion, pressing them against the side of the pan to leave behind as much oil as possible. Transfer the garlic and onion to a blender or food processor.

Add the chiles to the hot saucepan. Turn quickly as they fry, toast, and release a delicious aroma, about 30 seconds in all. Too much frying/toasting will make them bitter. Remove and drain on paper towels. Set the pan aside.

Add the tomatoes to the blender containing the garlic and onion and process to a smooth purée; strain the purée to get rid of the pieces of tomato skin if using fresh tomatoes. Heat the saucepan over medium-high heat. Add the purée and stir nearly constantly until it has thickened to the consistency of tomato paste, about 10 minutes. Add the broth and epazote and bring to a boil; then partially cover and gently simmer over medium to medium-low heat for 30 minutes. Taste and season with salt, usually 1/2 teaspoon, depending on the saltiness of your broth.

Divide the cheese and avocado among soup bowls. Ladle a portion of the broth into each bowl, top with a portion of the tortilla strips, and crumble on a little toasted chile. Carry these satisfying bowls of soup to the table and offer your guests wedges of lime to squeeze in to their liking.

roasted poblano guacamole
with garlic and parsley

Was there ever a fruit as sensual as an avocado? So rough-hewn, dare-to-touch-me masculine on the outside, so yielding, inviting, soft spring green and feminine inside? Writers have proclaimed that the avocado, tomato, and chile are among Mexico's gifts to the world. And they name guacamole, where all three come together, as a perfect work of art.

serves
6 as an appetizer, 8 to 10 as a nibble

2 medium fresh poblano chiles, about 6 ounces
1 ripe medium round or 2 plum tomatoes,
    about 6 ounces
2 garlic cloves, unpeeled
3 tablespoons chopped flat-leaf parsley
3 ripe medium-large avocados, about 1¼ pounds
1 teaspoon salt, or to taste
1 to 2 tablespoons fresh lime juice
2 tablespoons finely crumbled Mexican queso
    añejo or other dry grating cheese, such as
    Romano or Parmesan
a few slices of radish, for garnish

Arrange the poblano chiles, tomatoes and garlic on a baking sheet and place 4 inches below a very hot broiler. Roast, turning every couple of minutes, until the chiles and tomatoes are soft, blistered and blackened in spots and the garlic is soft, 12 to 13 minutes total. Place the chiles in a bowl and cover with a towel. Let stand for 5 minutes. Wipe off the blackened skin. Pull or cut out the stems, seed pods and seeds; rinse quickly to remove any stray seeds and bits of char. When the tomatoes are cool, peel off and discard their skins. Slip the papery skins off the garlic. Crush or process the garlic and chiles coarsely in a mortar or food processor, starting with the garlic; place in a large bowl. Drain and chop the roasted tomatoes and add to the poblano mixture along with the parsley.

Scoop the avocado flesh into a bowl and coarsely mash with a potato masher or the back of a large spoon.

Taste and season with the salt, then add enough lime juice to enliven all the flavors. Cover with plastic wrap, placing it directly on the surface, and refrigerate until you're ready to eat. To serve, scoop into a decorative bowl or Mexican mortar, sprinkle with the queso añejo, and stud with radish slices.

Working ahead: The roasted poblanos, tomatoes and garlic can be made a day or so in advance, but don't purée them until you are ready to make the guacamole. The flavor of the guacamole is enhanced if allowed to stand for 30 minutes before serving. Store for several hours, tightly covered, in the refrigerator; add the cheese and radish slices at the last moment.

quick-fried shrimp
with sweet toasty garlic

3/4 cup peeled whole garlic cloves (about 2 large heads)

1 cup extra-virgin olive oil

salt to taste

1 lime

2 canned chipotle chiles en adobo, seeded and cut into thin strips

2 pounds medium-large shrimp, peeled, leaving the last joint and tail intact if desired, about 48

3 tablespoons chopped fresh cilantro or parsley (optional)

2 limes, cut into wedges

The garlic in a perfect mojo de ajo is meltingly soft, having been prepared with enough good oil to have been cooked evenly and to pool luxuriously at the bottom of the plate. It's golden in color, sweet and nutty in flavor, and almost a touch gooey in texture. Since this is Mexican mojo (as opposed to Cuban mojo criollo, say), lime juice balances the garlic-oil richness, and a touch of red chile adds a little awe. Perfect seafood in mojo de ajo means perfectly fresh seafood, full of flavor and texture (no place for mild, wimpy, fine-flaked fish, in my opinion).

Chop or process the garlic with a sharp knife or in a food processor into 1/8-inch bits. You should have about 1/2 cup chopped garlic. Scoop into a 1-quart saucepan, measure in the oil (you need it all for even cooking) and 1/2 teaspoon salt and place over medium-low heat. Cook until there is just a hint of movement on the surface of the oil, stirring occasionally. Adjust the heat to the very lowest possible setting to keep the mixture at that very gentle simmer with bubbles rising in the pot like mineral water. Cook, stirring occasionally, until the garlic is tender and the color of light brown sugar, about 30 minutes; the slower the cooking, the sweeter the garlic.

Squeeze the juice of 1 lime into the pan and simmer until most of the juice has evaporated or been absorbed into the garlic, about 5 minutes. Stir in the chiles, then taste the mojo de ajo and add a little more salt if you think it needs it. Keep the pan over low heat so the garlic will be warm when the shrimp are ready.

Place a 12-inch nonstick skillet over medium-high heat and spoon in 1 1/2 tablespoons of the oil (but not the garlic) from the mojo. Add half of the shrimp to the skillet, sprinkle generously with salt, then stir gently and continuously until the shrimp are just cooked through,

3 or 4 minutes. Stir in the cilantro or parsley. Scoop the shrimp onto a deep serving platter. Repeat with the remaining half of the shrimp and another 1 1/2 tablespoons of the garlicky oil.

Use a slotted spoon to scoop out the warm bits of garlic and chiles from the pan and douse them over the shrimp. You may have as much as 1/3 cup of the oil left over, for which you'll be grateful—it's wonderful for sautéing practically anything. If you're a garlic lover, you're about to have the treat of your life, served with lime wedges to add sparkle. Serve with corn tortillas, tangy ceviche, asparagus vinaigrette and fruit, poached or in a tart. Don't forget a good bottle of white wine. Viognier is my favorite here.

Working ahead: The mojo de ajo keeps for a couple of weeks in the refrigerator (the oil will become solid but will liquefy again at room temperature), so I never recommend making a small amount. Mojo in the refrigerator represents great potential for a quick, wonderful meal. Warm cold mojo slowly before using. For the best texture, cook the shrimp immediately before serving. Or cook them several hours ahead, douse them with the garlic mojo and serve it all at room temperature.

tequila-flamed **mangoes**

serves **6**

4 medium ripe mangoes, about 3 pounds
$1/4$ cup ($1/2$ stick) butter
$1/2$ cup packed brown sugar
$1/4$ to $1/3$ cup tequila (with all the other flavors, a simple blanco tequila is fine here)
3 tablespoons sugar
1 cup homemade crema, crème fraîche or sour cream,
     or $1 1/2$ to 2 cups good vanilla ice cream

Peel the mangoes with a sharp paring knife, then cut the flesh from the pits, to which it clings tightly. Stand a mango on one end and slice the flesh from one side of the pit. Turn the mango around and slice the flesh from the other side. You'll be able to get a couple of thin slices of flesh off the pit on each end. Cut the large pieces into long $1/2$-inch-wide "fingers" or wedges.

Preheat the oven to 350 degrees. Place the butter in a 9×13-inch baking dish and place in the oven. When melted, about 5 minutes, remove from the oven and add the mango slices. Sprinkle with the brown sugar, stir gently to coat the mangoes completely, then spread out evenly in the dish. Bake, shaking the dish occasionally, for about 45 minutes; the mango juices will quickly seep out, then slowly simmer away, leaving you with toothsome mango slices that have a wonderfully concentrated flavor.

Pour the tequila into a small saucepan and set over low heat at serving time. Don't get the tequila too hot, or it won't flame. Sprinkle the mangoes evenly with the sugar, then lower the lights and get everyone's attention. Pour the tequila over the hot mangoes and immediately light it. Holding the baking dish with a towel or pot holder, shake it back and forth (this is for effect—it'll give you more dramatic flames). When the flames subside, spoon a portion of mangoes onto each of six dessert plates. Serve with a dollop of crema or ice cream.

Working ahead: The dish can be made successfully through baking. It's best finished and served within a few hours, though it can be covered and refrigerated for a day. Rewarm made-ahead mangoes before flaming.

Mangoes smell outlandishly enticing—at least to me. More than any other widely available tropical fruit, they carry the fully intense aroma that inhabits markets of torrid climes. Some find that fragrance a little reckless, verging on improper. Others—like me—feel it seduces like white truffles and saffron, creating a deep-down itch that's scratched only by consuming big mouthfuls of the perfumed substance. When the fruit is soft, but not mushy, and aromatic, it's ready to eat. Which is simply what most Mexicans do. On occasion, though, it's been known to show up amid show-stopping flames in dishes like this. The mangoes' texture firms to a delectable chewiness during the long baking. Plus, their flavor concentrates, giving them all the vitality they need to stand up to the tequila. And this is an easy dessert to do when you need something dramatic and special.

rafih**benjelloun**

Rafih Benjelloun has been a fixture in Atlanta since 1991, when he opened The Imperial Fez, recognized as one of the top Moroccan restaurants in the United States, with his wife, Rita.

Rafih was born in Fez, Morocco, and Rita in Marrakesh, and both studied culinary arts in Western Europe. Rafih began his career as a restaurateur in San Francisco and opened top restaurants in Denver and Boulder, Colorado. Following their marriage, Rafih and Rita established a top restaurant in Vail before arriving in Atlanta. Rafih has been recognized as one of the three top chefs in the Southeastern region and won the Chef's Award of Excellence in the Chef's Hall of Fame. He has also appeared on the cover of *Bon Appétit* and made an appearance on the Food Network's *My Country, My Kitchen*.

Rafih and Rita are active members of Les Toques Blanches, the Brotherhood of International Chefs. In addition, they place a very high priority on contributing to the community on local, national, and international levels. They are active participants and contributors to Operation Smile, Share Our Strength, the Atlanta Community Food Bank, African Children's Fund, and Hosea Feed the Hungry & Homeless.

...*our noses guide all our senses.*

As a chef cooking for the past thirty-six years, I have come to the conclusion that our noses guide all our senses. The Moroccan cuisine is all based on the quality of spices and fresh ingredients that give the true pleasure to eating. Some herbs and spices we use and serve in Morocco are called beldy, meaning true, old-fashioned, or organic. The Moroccan cumin is the most powerful of all cumin; just a few pinches will give you the strongest aroma and sharp flavors. It is sold at three or four times the price of the imported one, yet all good cooks will prefer the Moroccan cumin every time. When the spices we are about to use don't reveal the quality or the strength we need, it is recommended to toast the seeds gently for one to two minutes in a dry sauté pan to wake up the oils and aroma before grinding the spices. This will help you produce the bites that bite back.

Photographer: **jim**mcfarlane

Food Stylist: **caroline**westmore

briwatts with fruits

recipesrecipes

Briwatts with Fruits

Moroccan Marinated Baby Eggplant Salad

Lamb M'Rozia with Apples, Pears and Prunes with Honey and Almonds

rafih**benjelloun** 25

briwatts with fruits

serves **8 to 10**

1 cup diced strawberries
2 pears, diced
2 apples, diced
1 cup chocolate chips
1/2 cup coconut
1/2 cup roasted almonds, crushed
1/2 cup raisins
1 tablespoon cinnamon
pinch of cloves
pinch of nutmeg
1/4 cup condensed milk
2 tablespoons orange blossom water
10 sheets phyllo dough
1 cup (2 sticks) butter, melted
1/2 cup confectioners' sugar, for garnish
1 teaspoon cinnamon, for garnish

Combine the strawberries, pears, apples, chocolate chips, coconut, almonds, raisins, cinnamon, cloves, nutmeg, condensed milk and orange blossom water in a bowl; mix well.

Preheat the oven to 350 degrees. Cover the phyllo with a damp towel until ready to use so it won't dry out. Brush 1 sheet of the dough with butter. Fold the sheet in half diagonally, then in half again to form a triangle; press the edges to seal, place on a generously buttered baking sheet, and brush again with butter. Repeat with the remaining phyllo sheets.

Bake until golden brown.

Remove to a platter and top with the fruit mixture. Garnish with confectioners' sugar and a sprinkle of cinnamon. Serve hot.

moroccan marinated baby eggplant salad

serves **4 to 6**

8 to 12 baby eggplants
lemon juice and salt to taste
4 cups ginger juice
1 tablespoon paprika
1 tablespoon cumin
4 cloves garlic, finely chopped
4 stems parsley, finely chopped
4 stems cilantro, finely chopped
2 stems fresh oregano, finely chopped
2 stems fresh basil, finely chopped
juice of 1 lemon, or
    2 tablespoons red wine vinegar
2 tablespoons olive oil
1/4 teaspoon chile flakes
pinch of cayenne pepper
1/4 teaspoon cinnamon
1 teaspoon black pepper
salt to taste
lemon wedges, for garnish

Trim the baby eggplants and cut like flowers. Combine with water to cover in a large bowl and add lemon juice and salt to taste. Soak for 1 hour; drain. Bring 3 cups of the ginger juice to a boil in a large saucepan. Add the eggplants and cook for 20 to 25 minutes or until tender. Strain and let stand in the colander for 30 minutes to 1 hour.

Combine the eggplants with the remaining 1 cup ginger juice in a large bowl. Add the paprika, cumin, garlic, parsley, cilantro, oregano, basil, juice of 1 lemon, olive oil, chile flakes, cayenne pepper, cinnamon and black pepper. Season with salt and mix well. Store in the refrigerator.

Mix again at serving time. Remove the eggplants from the liquid with a slotted spoon and spoon around the serving plate. Garnish with lemon wedges and serve cold.

lamb m'rozia with apples, pears and prunes with honey and almonds

serves **8 to 10**

1 pound prunes
2 cups water
1 tablespoon sugar
1/4 cup olive oil
2 large onions, finely chopped
4 pounds bone-in lamb legs or shoulder,
   cut into chunks
1 cup finely chopped parsley
generous pinch of saffron
2 tablespoons ginger
1 teaspoon cinnamon

1/2 teaspoon nutmeg
pinch of ground cloves
1 teaspoon black pepper
salt to taste
3 cups water
4 apples, cut into 6 wedges
4 pears, cut into 6 wedges
1 cup raisins
1 1/2 cups honey
1/4 cup sesame seeds, for garnish
1 cup roasted almonds, for garnish

Combine the prunes with 2 cups water and the sugar in a saucepan and cook for 20 minutes.

Heat the olive oil in a heavy saucepan. Add the onions and sauté until tender. Add the lamb, parsley, saffron, ginger, cinnamon, nutmeg, cloves, black pepper, salt and 3 cups water. Cover and cook for about 45 minutes.

Remove the lamb to a platter and spoon some of the cooking liquid over it. Add the apples, pears, prune mixture and raisins to the saucepan. Cook for 10 minutes. Stir in the honey and cook for 3 to 5 minutes longer.

Remove the fruit to the serving platter with the lamb and spoon the sauce over the top. Garnish with the sesame seeds, almonds and additional fruits if desired. Serve hot.

carol**blomstrom**

As a computer person developing business systems software for over thirty years, Carol Blomstrom thought she knew a lot about business. But when she began operating Lotsa Pasta in the Pacific Beach area of San Diego in 1989, she realized she had lotsa learning to do.

Carol's original plan was to market fresh, handmade pastas and homemade sauces to take home and cook, similar to the way Mrs. Fields marketed cookies, using a sophisticated computer system that could track sales and inventory across a chain of retail stores. Carol's ambition was to own ninety-seven pasta retail stores. She jokes that she is only ninety-six stores short.

...only ninety-six stores short

The retail store offered twelve flavors of freshly made pasta in eight different shapes and eighteen freshly made pasta sauces. All kinds of entrées were offered, such as lasagna, chicken Parmesan, and ravioli. However, operating a retail store in that particularly "cooking-impaired" neighborhood was a challenge, so Carol added a restaurant component.

The restaurant has moved twice to larger locations, eventually expanding to 161 seats in the Pacific Plaza Shopping Center. Now Carol is happy being a full-time restaurateur. Ten years ago, she hired her son, Kirk, who now manages the back of the house. She enjoys working with family because it allows her to spend time with them. It reminds Carol of one of her favorite bumper stickers: "When your kids get nice to live with, they go live with someone else."

When she is not at the restaurant, Carol spends her time volunteering. She was awarded the title of Pacific Beach's Honorary Mayor for 2004. In the culinary world, she is on the board of the California Restaurant Association, San Diego Chapter, and the Southern California Culinary Guild. Carol is a member of Les Dames d'Escoffier and a member of IACP, serving as its Culinary Experience Committee Chair.

Photographer
jesseramirez

Food Stylist
katie**klarin**

garlic, scallion and parsley **pasta**

recipesrecipes

Garlic, Scallion and Parsley Pasta with Vodka Sauce

Artichoke Mousse

Mixed Greens with Shallot Vinaigrette

Citrus Granita

carol**blomstrom**

garlic, scallion and parsley
pasta with vodka sauce

When cooking pasta, I follow these steps. Heat the sauce in a large frying pan. Boil the water in a generous pasta pot. Add the pasta to the boiling water and cook either 30 or 90 seconds, depending on the cut. Drain the pasta and add immediately to the heated sauce. Toss the sauce and pasta together and heat another minute or two. Serve immediately.

Nothing tastes better than fresh pasta made with quality ingredients. In the restaurant, we use half semolina flour and half fancy durum flour, which are high-protein and high-gluten flours. Both are made from durum wheat, which is a winter wheat that is grown in an area where the ground freezes in the winter. I have substituted all-purpose flour in this recipe for convenience. I have made it with all-purpose flour in the classroom many times, and the results are great.

The vodka sauce is the most popular sauce at Lotsa Pasta. It is rich and yummy and well worth a splurge every once in a while. It has been a family favorite for many years. When we make this recipe in the restaurant, at the end of the cooking, we attempt to light the top of the batch to ensure that all of the alcohol has been cooked off. Beware that red chile pepper flakes vary in heat. You may want to decrease or increase the amount of chile flakes for your taste.

serves 8

9 large garlic cloves
2 medium scallions
5 stems parsley
3 1/2 cups unbleached all-purpose flour
3 large eggs
vodka sauce

Combine the garlic, scallions and parsley in a blender and purée as finely as possible. Measure the flour into the mixing bowl of a stand mixer and add the eggs and puréed vegetables. Using the paddle attachment, mix until the ingredients are incorporated and a ball is formed, about 1 to 2 minutes. Change to the dough hook and continue to knead the dough for 10 minutes. Wrap the dough in plastic and allow to rest for 1 hour in the refrigerator.

Divide the dough into 4 pieces so it will be easier to work with. Cover the dough that is not being used so it will not dry out. Attach the pasta roller attachment to the stand mixer. Begin passing the pasta through the rollers, beginning with the widest setting, Number 1, then passing it again through settings 2, 3, 4, 5 and continuing to number 6 or 7, depending on your preference for pasta thickness.

When you have finished rolling out the pasta, attach the angel hair or fettuccini pasta cutter and cut the pasta into ribbons. Toss the pasta ribbons in extra flour to prevent them from sticking together.

Cook the fresh pasta in plenty of boiling water; angel hair takes 30 seconds and fettuccini takes 90 seconds to cook to al dente. Serve with vodka sauce or your favorite sauce.

vodka sauce
1 cup vodka
1 tablespoon crushed red chile pepper flakes
1/2 cup (1 stick) butter
1 quart heavy whipping cream
1 (28-ounce) can quality canned tomatoes, puréed in a blender
1 cup (4 ounces) grated Parmesan cheese

Combine the vodka and red chile pepper flakes in a cup and soak for about 1 hour to infuse the flavor into the vodka. Pour the vodka mixture into a medium saucepan and bring to a boil. Boil for 5 minutes or until the alcohol has evaporated. Add the butter and cook until melted.

Add the cream and tomatoes and bring to a boil. Reduce the heat and simmer for 5 minutes. Whisk in the Parmesan cheese. I like to top this pasta with a grilled chicken breast marinated in Italian dressing.

artichoke mousse

This mousse keeps well in the refrigerator for over a week. It is one of my favorite recipes, and I serve it several ways. Sometimes I serve it on baked potatoes or hot pasta. To serve it cold, I use a very small ice cream scoop and place a mound on rice crackers and garnish by sprinkling the top with finely minced chives. I garnish the serving plate with very thin slices of lemon, cut into halves, as a scallop pattern on the outer edge of the serving plate. To serve it hot, I place the mousse in a two-cup ovenproof dish and heat it at 350 degrees until hot and lightly brown on top, about fifteen minutes. It can be served with rice crackers, your favorite crackers, and/or slices of cucumbers.

serves **8**

1 (8^1/2-ounce) can artichoke hearts or bottoms
^{1}/2 cup mayonnaise
^{1}/2 cup (2 ounces) freshly grated
  Parmesan cheese
^{1}/2 cup (2 ounces) shredded mozzarella cheese
^{1}/4 cup thinly sliced green onions
1 teaspoon freshly ground black pepper
^{1}/4 teaspoon dried tarragon, crushed
^{1}/4 teaspoon cayenne pepper
salt to taste

Drain the artichoke hearts or bottoms and squeeze well with your hands, pressing out as much moisture as possible. Place the drained artichokes in a food processor fitted with a steel blade. Process until very finely chopped.

Combine the artichokes with the mayonnaise, Parmesan cheese, mozzarella cheese, green onions, black pepper, tarragon, cayenne pepper and salt in a bowl and mix thoroughly.

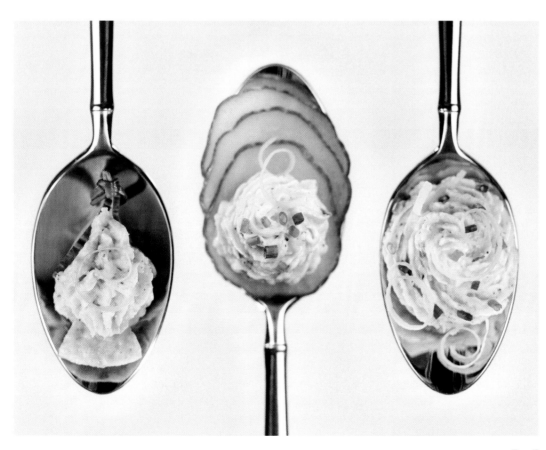

mixed greens with shallot vinaigrette

This salad is so delicious and so simple. It mixes salty bacon, creamy Gorgonzola cheese, and crunchy roasted hazelnuts with a tangy shallot vinaigrette. It always gets compliments. This is a menu component that you can prepare ahead and toss at the last minute. I like this recipe so much that we recently added it to our restaurant menu, where it is very popular.

serves **8**

1 cup minced shallots
$1/2$ cup crumbled crisp-cooked bacon
$1/2$ cup red wine vinegar
$1^1/2$ cups extra-virgin olive oil
2 (5-ounce) packages mixed baby greens or
     herb salad mix
1 cup hazelnuts, roasted and skins removed
1 cup (4 ounces) crumbled Gorgonzola cheese

Mix the shallots, bacon, vinegar and olive oil in a bowl. Chill in the refrigerator for 8 hours or longer to meld the flavors.

Toss the vinaigrette with the mixed greens in a bowl. Spoon onto serving plates and top with the hazelnuts and Gorgonzola cheese.

These recipes make up a typical and comforting family meal. They are relatively simple, and most have parts that can be made ahead of time so that they come together easily when it is time for dinner. They are also recipes that have lotsa flavor and relatively few ingredients. All of them are on the menu at Lotsa Pasta.

citrus granita

Granita is defined as frozen fruit juices. If made in an ice cream maker, there is more air introduced, and the result is lighter. It originally was made by placing the liquid in a shallow pan in the freezer, then stirring it every 15 minutes until frozen. This recipe is always a big hit and very refreshing after a heavy meal. I save the grapefruit halves after squeezing the juice and removing all the pulp to serve as containers for the presentation of the citrus granita.

serves 8

4 cups sugar
4 cups water
3 cups freshly squeezed grapefruit juice
2 cups unsweetened pineapple juice
1 cup freshly squeezed lime juice
1/2 cup freshly squeezed lemon juice

grated zest of 3 limes
grated zest of 1 lemon
1/4 cup white tequila
grapefruit shells (optional)
lime slices or lime leaves, for garnish

Bring the sugar and water to a boil in a large saucepan and simmer for 5 minutes, or until the mixture has a syrupy consistency. Cool to room temperature. Add the grapefruit juice, pineapple juice, lime juice, lemon juice, lime zest and lemon zest to the syrup. Stir in the tequila. Chill in the refrigerator; the mixture should be as cold as possible before freezing.

Place the liquid in an ice cream freezer. Freeze according to the manufacturer's instructions. Transfer to a container and store in the freezer. Spoon into the grapefruit halves to serve and garnish with lime slices or lime leaves.

You can also freeze this in the freezer by the method described above.

margarita**carrillo de salinas**

In my heart, there is a little corner that belongs to the kitchen where I nest my family values, the hard and honest work that was taught to me, the echoes of the long, intimate conversations with my family while all of us were cooking, cooking the scent of life.

Born in Mexico into a family with a strong cooking tradition, Salinas originally received a Bachelor of Arts in Education from the National University of Mexico. She has studied cuisine at the Culinary Institute of America and Le Cordon Bleu, among others, as well as in Mexico. She has spent more than twenty years researching, studying, teaching, and cooking Mexican cuisines. Salinas is currently chef of the Ministry of Agriculture in Mexico and also the executive chef of Il Ricco restaurant in Mexico City. She co-owns and is executive chef of two additional restaurants in Los Cabos, BCS, Mexico, and owns an artisanal ice cream factory, Finno Gelatto Magnifico. She has worked to improve conditions for women working in restaurant kitchens in Mexico. She holds memberships in many professional organizations, including Slow Food and IACP, where she has been Country Coordinator since 2001.

In my heart...I nest my family values ...the scent of life.

My life has been woven between pots and pans; the best, most important memories have to do with spending time in the kitchen, with tumultuous family lunches and the aroma of home-cooked meals. Life revolved around that room because, in my family, cooking is an art that has been handed down from generation to generation. It represents the hard work and devotion, creativity and research of generous women. Cooking ability is coveted by those who can't cook but love to eat and is the pride of men in the family, who truly consider it an asset. I believe in the tradition of cooking, the importance it has in the history and identity of a family, of a country. It's part of the bond that ties us together as people, a speechless way of communicating love, interest, and devotion, a way to remain and leave a footstep in this world we live in.

Photographer
dawnsmith

Food Stylist
melanie**dubberly**

cold chicken cooked in vinaigrette

recipesrecipes

Cold Chicken Cooked in Vinaigrette

Pineapple and Sweet Potato Dessert

margarita**carrillo de salinas** 35

cold chicken cooked in vinaigrette

Nowadays, when I recall family dinners and gatherings, I recognize them as a concept of family generosity, of love, of life vibrating and spinning around traditions and food. Someday, my kitchen will be the one in my children's memories. It'll be a place filled with life, proteins and memories, carbohydrates and experiences, the place in which we all talked about our feelings and our destiny and where they learned about generosity. When they remember our dishes, they'll recognize the essence of ourselves, our culture, and even our religion.

serves 4

6 chicken feet, manicured
1 (3-pound) chicken, cut into pieces
  and skinned
2 bay leaves
1 sprig thyme
1 sprig marjoram
1 garlic head, cut into halves crosswise
1 large onion, thickly sliced

8 black peppercorns
1 tiny chunk of nutmeg
1 cup cider vinegar
1 cup olive oil
1 cup white wine or cider
salt to taste
chopped parsley or pickled jalapeños,
  for garnish

Arrange the chicken feet in a 4-quart clay or stainless steel pot with a lid. Arrange the chicken with alternate layers of the bay leaves, thyme, marjoram, garlic, onion, peppercorns and nutmeg in the pot. Add the vinegar, olive oil and wine; season with salt. Place in the refrigerator for 8 hours or longer. If using a clay pot, let stand at room temperature for 1 hour.

Cook the chicken over low heat for about 2 hours. Remove from the heat and adjust the seasonings. Remove the chicken to a dish and strain the cooking liquid into the dish. Cover and chill for 5 hours or until the juices set.

Garnish with chopped parsley and serve cold in the aspic with potato salad. You may also serve hot with rice pilaf and pickled jalapeños.

Scents take me back in time. With them, nostalgic evocations come to my mind, filled with beautiful images, colored with aromas, sounds, dishes. Whenever a smell hits me, it drags me to the gardens of my childhood. The smell of freshly brewed coffee reminds me of breakfast with my dad and having to wake up earlier so we could all eat together before the dairy duties. In my heart, there is a little corner that belongs to the kitchen where I nest my family values, the hard and honest work that was taught to me, the echoes of the long, intimate conversations with my family while all of us were cooking, cooking the scent of life.

A certain and indescribable smell reminds me of my mother, always in high heels, cooking for us with a smile. She was essential in my culinary involvement, but my inspiration and guide was my grandmother. I waited anxiously for summertime, when she organized cooking lessons for her granddaughters. There, she taught me the basics, and then piqued my curiosity and my creativity. She was a positive, energetic woman, very conservative, very innovative, extremely fierce, courageous, and wonderfully patient. It was through her that I discovered myself as a chef.

pineapple and sweet potato dessert

serves 12

2 pounds yellow sweet potatoes
1 large (3-pound) pineapple
2 (3-inch) cinnamon sticks
1 cup sugar
4 ounces slivered roasted almonds, for garnish

Cook the sweet potatoes until tender; peel and mash in a bowl. Peel, core and finely chop the pineapple, reserving the juice. Combine the pineapple, reserved pineapple juice, cinnamon sticks and sugar in a 4-quart stainless steel saucepan. Cook over medium heat, stirring occasionally, until tender and juicy, about 20 minutes.

Add the sweet potatoes and cook until the mixture is stiff enough that you can see the bottom of the saucepan when the mixture is stirred. Cool to room temperature and remove the cinnamon sticks.

Chill until serving time. Spoon into small dessert bowls or martini glasses and garnish with the almonds.

My childhood memories are filled with images of family, setting the table, cooking with wooden spoons, teaching me and my cousins, telling us that well-known phrase, "the way to a man's heart is through his stomach"—not very popular with the feminist movement, but extremely accurate in countries where family is still the operative word. My father's encouragement and willingness to eat anything my sister and I cooked can't be forgotten. I picture him saying lovingly, "Well, if something goes wrong with your cake, it's just eggs and sugar; surely you can try again."

kaspar**donier**

My love of food began in Switzerland, where I grew up and was fortunate enough to have a "foodie" upbringing. We grew, raised, and made so much of our food ourselves. Even the kids helped out and were involved in food preparation.

Kaspar Donier was born in Davos, Switzerland, and, at the age of sixteen, began his formal training as a chef apprentice at the Hilton Hotel in Zurich. In 1976, Donier left Switzerland to become chef garde manger, then chef saucier at the Hilton Hotel in Vancouver, Canada. He moved in 1980 to Vancouver's Four Seasons Hotel and was soon promoted to sous chef and, in 1983, executive sous chef. In 1985, Donier transferred to Houston's Inn on the Park, Four Seasons, and was promoted to executive chef the following year.

Since May 1989, Donier and his wife, Nancy, have operated Kaspar's in Seattle, using Donier's extensive travels and work experience to create a contemporary cuisine that combines the Northwest style of fresh seafood and produce with classic French, Oriental, and Southwestern seasonings and techniques to create a contemporary Pacific Northwest cuisine.

Every year since opening, Kaspar's has placed in local and national top restaurant lists, earning Best View Restaurant in the Pacific Northwest, Best Business Lunch in the Pacific Northwest, Best Kept Secret in the State of Washington, and Best Chocolate Dessert. Kaspar's was also named by *Gourmet* magazine, *USA Today*, *Money* magazine, and the *New York Times* as one of the top regional restaurants in the Pacific Northwest. Chef Donier and Kaspar's have been featured on national radio and television, and Donier was nominated for the James Beard Foundation Award as America's Best Chef: Northwest for four years. He has also been inducted into the International Association of Maitres-Conceils in French gastronomy. He is active in the Seattle Food Lifeline and End Hunger networks, the Pike Place Market Foundation, and many community and charitable efforts.

Photographer
dianepadys

Food Stylist
christy**nordstrom**

*...a contemporary Pacific
Northwest cuisine*

asian **duck** confit

recipesrecipes

Asian Duck Confit

Oriental Crispy Fried Asparagus

Dungeness Crab Hash Cakes with Sun-Dried Tomato and Basil Sauce

Cherry Cabernet Tiramisu

asian duck **confit**

serves **6**

6 duck legs with thighs
3 green onions, coarsely chopped
1 medium yellow onion, coarsely chopped
2 tablespoons coarsely chopped fresh ginger
3 garlic cloves
1 teaspoon chile flakes
$1/4$ cup soy sauce

1 tablespoon sesame oil
3 tablespoons oyster sauce
$1/4$ cup honey
1 cup sherry
$1/2$ stalk lemon grass
4 cups water

Remove the skin and trim the fat from the duck. Combine the green onions, yellow onion, ginger, garlic, chile flakes, soy sauce, sesame oil, oyster sauce, honey, sherry, lemon grass and water in a large pot and bring to a boil.

Add the duck and return to a boil. Reduce the heat and simmer for approximately $1^{1}/2$ to $1^{3}/4$ hours or until the meat separates from the bone.

Remove the duck from the broth with a slotted spoon and transfer to another pan. Skim any remaining fat from the broth, then strain into the pan with the duck and reheat to serve. Serve with shiitake leek couscous, fried rice or crunchy Asian vegetables.

This recipe can be prepared one day ahead. Store the duck in the refrigerator and skim the fat from the top again before reheating.

What we didn't prepare or grow ourselves, we fished, hunted, or found. My father was a hunter of deer, elk, chamois, and hare. We caught trout and Northern pike on outings to the local rivers and lakes. We collected hazelnuts from the bushes alongside the logging roads. We foraged for wild mushrooms, mostly chanterelles and porcini mushrooms, and many more that we had inspected by the town's mushroom expert.

oriental crispy **fried asparagus**

serves 4

oil for deep-frying
1 bunch small asparagus
3 tablespoons buttermilk
1 teaspoon soy sauce

2 teaspoons hoisin sauce
1/3 cup flour
1/3 cup cornstarch
2 tablespoons sesame seeds

Preheat a deep fryer filled with oil. Trim the bottom 2 inches from the asparagus stalks. Mix the buttermilk, soy sauce and hoisin sauce in a shallow bowl. Add the asparagus and toss to coat.

Combine the flour, cornstarch and sesame seeds in a plastic bag. Add the asparagus to the bag and shake to coat well.

Add the asparagus to the heated oil and deep-fry for 2 to 4 minutes or until golden brown and crisp. Drain on paper towels. Serve with dips or prosciutto or as a side dish for fish or prawns.

You can reserve the trimmed asparagus bottoms for soups.

My grandfather made hard cider from the apples in his little orchard, which I helped to pick. My dad had lots of hobbies, including beekeeping. In the cold of early spring, we fed them with sugar syrup, and in the fall, hopefully, we would harvest plenty of honey, enough to last through the winter months.

dungeness crab hash cakes
with sun-dried tomato and basil sauce

serves **6**

2 medium russet potatoes, about 1 pound
1/2 pound Dungeness crab meat, cleaned
salt and pepper to taste
1/2 cup olive oil
1/2 cup white wine
1 garlic clove, chopped
1/4 cup chopped red onion
1 1/2 ounces sun-dried tomatoes, chopped
1/2 cup chicken stock
1 cup whipping cream
8 basil leaves

Bring a large pot of salted water to a boil. Add the potatoes and boil until tender. Peel the potatoes and grate coarsely with a cheese grater. Cool completely in the refrigerator, overnight for best results.

Mix the potatoes with the crab meat in a bowl and season with salt and pepper. Divide into 6 balls and flatten to form patties. Heat the olive oil in a frying pan. Add the crab hash cakes and fry for about 4 to 5 minutes per side, or until golden brown.

Combine the wine, garlic, onion and sun-dried tomatoes in a saucepan and cook until the wine is reduced by half. Add the chicken stock and cream and continue simmering until reduced by half, or to the desired consistency. Chop 4 of the basil leaves and add to the sauce. Season with salt and pepper.

Spoon some of the sauce onto each serving plate and top with a crab hash cake. Garnish with the remaining basil leaves.

I earned pocket money by keeping thirty to forty rabbits at a time, which my father then butchered. There was no local farmer's market, but there was a lot of food exchanging between neighbors. The growing season was short for our vegetable garden. We had potatoes, root vegetables for roasting, and hardy greens. A lot of canning and freezing was done for the long winter months.

Every Sunday morning, there was homemade zopf, a braided yeast bread, on the breakfast table, and each Saturday, we prepared a cake or pie just for the family or in case friends or relatives dropped in.

cherry cabernet tiramisu

This is made with a génoise, a rich, light cake made with flour, sugar, and eggs. It is similar to a sponge cake and was developed in Genoa, Italy.

serves 12 to 16

6 large eggs, separated
1 1/2 cups sugar
1 1/2 cups all-purpose flour
cherry compote
cream cheese frosting
rainier cherry sorbet
chocolate-covered cherries, chocolate shavings
    or mint sprigs

Preheat the oven to 350 degrees. Line a 12×16-inch baking sheet or jelly roll pan with parchment paper.

Place the egg yolks in an electric mixing bowl. Add 1/2 cup of the sugar gradually, beating until light and fluffy and pale yellow in color.

Beat the egg whites with the remaining sugar in a separate bowl until stiff. Fold half of the egg whites into the egg yolk mixture, alternating with sifting half the flour over the egg yolk mixture with a sieve or flour sifter. Fold in gently with a rubber spatula. Repeat the process with the remaining egg whites and flour.

Spread evenly in the prepared pan. Bake for 20 to 25 minutes or until the top is light brown and a toothpick inserted in the center comes out clean. Cool on a wire rack.

Cut the génoise crosswise into halves. Place a cake layer on a serving platter or plate. Drain the cherry compote, reserving the poaching liquid. Drizzle half the poaching liquid on the bottom layer of cake. Spread half the cream cheese frosting on top. Sprinkle the drained cherry compote on top of the cream cheese frosting.

Drizzle the remaining poaching liquid on the other half of the cake. Place the cake layer on top of the cherry compote, making sure the soaked layer is bottom side down. Spread the remaining cream cheese frosting on top. Refrigerate the tiramisu for several hours. Cut the tiramisu and serve with the cherry sorbet. Add chocolate-covered cherries, chocolate shavings or mint sprigs.

cherry compote
1 pound Bing cherries
1/2 lemon
1/2 cup water
1/2 cup sugar
1/4 cup cabernet sauvignon

Stem and pit the cherries; remove the peel from the lemon with a vegetable peeler. Combine the cherries, lemon peel, water, sugar and wine in a saucepan. Bring to a simmer and simmer for 10 minutes. Spoon into a small bowl and chill in the refrigerator.

cream cheese frosting
2 cups cabernet sauvignon
1 cup sugar
16 ounces cream cheese, softened

Pour the wine into a noncorrosive pan. Add the sugar and bring to a simmer. Simmer until reduced to 1 cup. Chill on ice or in the refrigerator.

Pulse the softened cream cheese in a food processor until smooth. Add the wine reduction with the machine running and pulse until smooth. Transfer to a bowl and refrigerate until ready to assemble.

rainier cherry sorbet
1 pound Rainier cherries, pitted
1/2 cup sugar

Process the cherries and sugar in a food processor or blender for about 3 minutes or until the mixture is very smooth. Transfer the cherry purée into an ice cream maker and freeze according to the manufacturer's directions.

We went on an outing to the mountaintops every September, walking two hours to pick wild blueberries. The hardest work we did was for wild strawberries, which took about two hours of picking to harvest three pints of berries, but it was worth it to taste them with fresh whipped cream.

tom**douglas**

Never having attended a culinary school, Tom's cooking knowledge comes mostly from dining out across America and Europe, using his "taste memory" to re-create and develop recipes in his own style.

A Delaware native, Tom Douglas started cooking at the Hotel DuPont in Wilmington, Delaware, before heading west to Seattle in 1978. From house-building to wine-selling to railroad car repair, Tom tried his hand at several jobs before settling on the restaurant business as his final career choice. Starting with the acclaimed Café Sport in 1984, Tom's cuisine helped define the Northwest style. His creativity with local ingredients and his respect for Seattle's ethnic traditions have earned his four restaurants a place on the national culinary map.

In November 1989, Douglas left the comfortable confines of Café Sport to start Dahlia Lounge, which soon became one of the Northwest's premier restaurants. Tom won the James Beard Foundation Award for Best Chef: Northwest in 1994. The Dahlia moved in May 2001 to a newly renovated building just one block up the street from the original location on Fourth Avenue, and Tom's retail bakery, Dahlia Bakery, opened in 2001.

In February 1995, Tom and Jackie Cross, his wife and business partner, opened their second restaurant, Etta's, named after their daughter, Loretta. It allows Tom to showcase his unique cooking style, using the best seafood available. They opened Palace Kitchen in March 1996, offering a menu more rustic in style, with a wood-fired grill offering nightly rotisserie specials. It was nominated by the James Beard Foundation as one of the country's Best New Restaurants in 1996. Lola, Tom, and Jackie's fourth restaurant opened in July 2004 with a Greek-inspired menu, combining local Northwest ingredients with Mediterranean freshness and simplicity.

Tom Douglas' Catering and Events offers Tom's catering clients the same outstanding experiences they have come to expect in his restaurants, while Tom Douglas' "Rub with Love" spice rubs and sauces let cooks exercise their own kitchen creativity. His first cookbook, *Tom Douglas' Seattle Kitchen*, was honored with a James Beard Foundation Award for Best Americana Cookbook. His second book, *Tom's Big Dinners*, features his secrets for home entertaining.

Photographer
toddtrice

Food Stylist
danmacey

grilled **prawn kebabs**

*...respect for Seattle's
ethnic traditions*

t
d

recipesrecipes

grilled prawn kebabs
with curried muscat glaze

At Lola, we serve these kebabs over a bed of charred onion, lemon, and fennel in a hot metal pan, and while they're still sizzling, we splash them with a little ouzo. Verjus, used in the glaze, means "green juice"; it is the tart juice of unripe wine grapes. You can buy verjus at some gourmet supermarkets.

serves 6

24 large prawns (about 1 1/4 pounds),
   peeled with the tails on and deveined
6 (10-inch) bamboo skewers, soaked in
   cold water for 30 minutes and drained
kosher salt and freshly ground black pepper
   to taste
olive oil for grilling
curried muscat glaze

curried muscat glaze
1/2 pound green seedless grapes
2 tablespoons verjus
1 3/4 teaspoons mild curry paste
1 1/2 teaspoons chopped shallot
1/4 teaspoon peeled and grated fresh ginger
3/4 cup white wine
2 tablespoons sugar

Fire up the grill. Thread 4 prawns onto each skewer and season them with salt and pepper. Set them aside on a large plate.

Brush the prawns and the grill with olive oil. Grill the kebabs, uncovered, over direct heat, turning them as needed, until cooked through, about 4 minutes, and brushing them twice on both sides with the curried muscat glaze. Remove the kebabs from the grill, place them on plates, and immediately brush each kebab with some of the remaining glaze. Serve immediately, accompanied by greek spaghetti (page 48) and horta if desired.

Purée the grapes, verjus, curry paste, shallot and ginger in a food processor or blender until smooth; you'll be able to get this a little smoother in a blender. Transfer the mixture to a heavy nonreactive saucepan and add the wine and sugar. Bring to a boil over medium-high heat and boil, stirring as needed, until the glaze is thick and reduced, about 10 minutes or more; you should have about 1/2 cup glaze, and it should be almost as thick as apple-sauce. Remove from the heat and set aside.

spicy sumac **carrot purée**

Serve this and a yogurt tzatziki in colorful bowls surrounded by pita wedges on a platter for your guests to share. The sumac used in this recipe is a dried red berry that is sold ground. It has a fruity, lemony flavor and is frequently used in Middle Eastern cooking. You can find sumac in well-stocked spice markets, or you can order online from www.worldspice.com.

serves **6 as an appetizer**

1^1/$_2$ pounds carrots, peeled and cut into
    1-inch chunks (if your carrots are thick,
    also cut them into halves lengthwise)
2^1/$_4$ teaspoons ground sumac
2^1/$_4$ teaspoons toasted and ground caraway
    seeds (see note)
1^1/$_4$ teaspoons toasted and ground cumin seeds
    (see note)
^{1}/$_4$ teaspoon cayenne, or to taste
2 tablespoons fresh lemon juice
^{1}/$_4$ cup extra-virgin olive oil
kosher salt to taste

Bring a pot of salted water to a boil and add the carrots. Reduce the heat slightly and simmer until the carrots are tender enough to crush with a spoon, about 25 to 30 minutes. Drain the carrots, then return them to the pot and heat over medium-high heat for a few minutes, shaking the pan, to evaporate any remaining water. Remove from the heat.

Purée the carrots with the sumac, caraway seeds, cumin seeds, cayenne and lemon juice in a food processor. Add the olive oil and pulse a few more times or until nearly smooth with a little texture. Season with salt.

Transfer to a small serving bowl and allow to cool to room temperature, or cover and refrigerate until needed.

Note: To toast whole spices, place them in a heavy skillet over medium heat for a few minutes until they are lightly browned and aromatic, stirring occasionally and watching carefully so they don't burn.

To grind spices, allow the toasted spices to cool slightly, then grind them in a spice grinder. We use a clean electric coffee bean grinder. For this recipe, combine the cumin and caraway seeds and toast and grind them together.

grandma dot's
greek spaghetti

This is the Greek recipe that my wife Jackie's mom and Loretta's grandmother, Dot, frequently prepared for Saturday night supper. Don't be afraid to get the butter quite dark; otherwise, Dot says that the pasta will be too greasy. The mizithra is a dry, salty, Greek sheep's milk cheese.

serves 6 to 8

1 1/2 pounds uncooked spaghetti
3/4 cup (1 1/2 sticks) unsalted butter
1 cup plus 2 tablespoons grated mizithra cheese

1 cup plus 2 tablespoons grated Parmesan cheese
kosher salt and freshly ground black pepper
2 tablespoons chopped parsley

Bring a large pot of salted water to a boil. Add the spaghetti and cook until al dente, about 11 minutes. Melt the butter in a small heavy saucepan over medium heat. Cook the butter until it foams and turns dark brown, about 5 to 10 minutes. Remove from the heat.

Drain the cooked spaghetti and return it to the pot. Add the browned butter and cheeses. Season with salt and pepper, keeping in mind that the mizithra is quite salty, and toss. Transfer to a platter or divide among individual plates, sprinkle the parsley on top, and serve immediately.

turnover pastry

serves 6

2 1/2 cups all-purpose flour
2 tablespoons sugar
1 teaspoon kosher salt

1 cup (2 sticks) unsalted butter, chilled
    and cut into pieces
6 to 8 tablespoons ice water, or more
    as needed

Place the flour, sugar and salt in a food processor and pulse to mix. Add the cold butter all at once and pulse a few times until the butter and flour form crumbs. Transfer the mixture to a bowl and start adding the ice water, 1 or 2 tablespoons at a time, mixing with a fork or rubber spatula and adding only as much water as needed for the dough to hold together when a clump is gently pressed between your fingers. Dump the dough out onto a large piece of plastic wrap. Use the plastic wrap to gather the dough together and force it into a flattened round. Chill, wrapped in plastic wrap, about 1 hour or longer before rolling it out.

Place the dough on a lightly floured work surface and cut into halves. Roll half of the dough at a time into a rough circle about 1/8 inch thick with a floured rolling pin. Cut each dough circle into 9 or 10 circles with a 4-inch biscuit cutter, setting them aside on a piece of parchment or waxed paper.

You can make the pastry dough a day or two ahead and keep it wrapped and refrigerated, or the dough can be kept frozen for a few weeks. Thaw frozen dough several hours or overnight before using. You can roll the dough out and cut it into circles several hours ahead. Put the pastry circles on a parchment-lined baking sheet, cover them loosely with a piece of plastic wrap, and refrigerate until you are ready to use them.

sweet goat cheese turnovers
with honey, pistachios and mint

Frying these turnovers in olive oil makes them extra delicious—and very Greek. Be sure to use pure olive oil for frying, not extra-virgin, because it has a higher smoking point. You can assemble the turnovers up to one day ahead and place them, uncooked, on vegetable oil-sprayed, parchment-lined baking pans. Cover them with plastic wrap and refrigerate until you are ready to fry them. You can also fry them several hours ahead and set them aside at room temperature. Reheat them in a 400-degree oven until they're hot, about 5 minutes.

serves **6**

1/2 cup chopped pistachios
8 ounces soft fresh goat cheese
1 tablespoon heavy cream
5 tablespoons sugar
2 teaspoons grated lemon zest
1 large egg yolk

1 tablespoon water
18 to 20 circles turnover pastry (page 48)
pure olive oil for frying
1/3 cup flavorful honey, or to taste
1/2 cup fresh mint leaves

Toast the pistachios on a baking sheet in a preheated 350- to 375-degree oven for 5 to 10 minutes, stirring occasionally and watching carefully so they don't burn. Beat the goat cheese with the cream, sugar and lemon zest in a bowl using a rubber spatula or wooden spoon. Beat the egg yolk and water in a small bowl with a fork just until combined for the egg wash.

Arrange the pastry circles on a lightly floured work surface. Spoon a heaping teaspoon of the goat cheese filling in the center of each circle. Brush the egg wash around the edge of each circle with a pastry brush. Fold over to form a half-moon turnover, pressing with a fork to seal the edges. Arrange the turnovers on parchment-lined baking pans sprayed with vegetable oil spray to prevent sticking, or use a flexible nonstick baking sheet, such as a Silpat, and you won't need to spray it.

Fill a wide, heavy, straight-sided pan with olive oil to a depth of at least 1 inch; the pan should be deep enough so it is not filled more than halfway with oil. Heat the oil to between 325 and 350 degrees, checking the temperature on a deep-frying thermometer. Fry the turnovers, in batches as necessary, turning to brown both sides. If your oil is too hot, the turnovers may brown before the dough is cooked through; it should take at least 3 minutes to brown a turnover on both sides. You may want to cut a turnover open and check that the dough is thoroughly cooked by the time it is browned. If the turnovers are browning too fast, turn the heat down a little. As the turnovers are browned, remove them with a slotted spoon or skimmer and drain on paper towels.

Arrange the turnovers on a large platter or individual plates. Drizzle them with the honey and sprinkle with the pistachios. Tear the mint leaves into pieces and scatter them over the top. Serve immediately.

toddenglish

Todd English graduated with honors from the Culinary Institute of America and honed his craft with Jean Jacques Rachou in New York and later in Italy, where he drew from his Italian heritage to develop his unique style and approach to cooking.

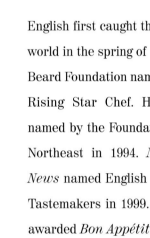

English first caught the eyes of the culinary world in the spring of 1991, when the James Beard Foundation named him their National Rising Star Chef. He was subsequently named by the Foundation as the Best Chef: Northeast in 1994. *Nation's Restaurant News* named English one of their Top Fifty Tastemakers in 1999. In 2001, English was awarded *Bon Appétit's* Restaurateur of the Year award. He was inducted into the James Beard Foundation's Who's Who of Food and Beverage in America in 2004.

Todd is the chef and owner of Olives in Charlestown, Massachusetts. Olives opened in April 1989 and has drawn acclaim for English's interpretive rustic Mediterranean cuisine. There are now additional locations in New York, Las Vegas, Washington, D.C., Aspen, and Tokyo.

English also has four Figs restaurants in the greater Boston area and two locations at LaGuardia Airport, serving traditional and eclectic pizzas and handmade pastas. He also has Tuscany at Mohegan Sun in Connecticut, which serves Italian-inspired foods; Bonfire, a steakhouse in Boston's Park Plaza Hotel that is a celebration of ranch cooking around the world; Kingfish Hall in Boston's Historic Faneuil Hall; and Fish Club at the Seattle Marriott Waterfront. Opened in early 2004, the Cunard Line's *Queen Mary 2* houses the restaurant Todd English, and Orlando hosts bluezoo at the Walt Disney World Resort's Dolphin Hotel.

The original Olives was voted Best New Restaurant by *Boston Magazine*. Since then, it has been honored as Best Food and Top Table by *Gourmet* and is consistently named Boston's #1 Favorite Restaurant by the *Zagat Survey*. Figs was given the Hot Concept award from *Nation's Restaurant News*. Kingfish Hall was named Best of Boston by *Travel & Leisure* magazine.

English has a public television series, *Cooking In with Todd English,* and has made appearances on many other television programs. He has authored the critically acclaimed cookbooks *The Olives Table*, *The Figs Table*, and *The Olives Dessert Table* and is involved in several charities.

ugly **monkfish** hobo pack

Photographer
jim**scherer**

Food Stylist
marie**piraino**

Cooking is a comfort, an art, and a celebration of love, family, and prosperity.

recipesrecipes

Ugly Monkfish Hobo Pack

Peach Shortcake with Bourbon

ugly monkfish hobo pack

serves 2 to 4

1 whole monkfish, head removed,
    skinned and cleaned
1 teaspoon ground cumin
1 teaspoon ground turmeric
2 teaspoons salt
1 teaspoon black pepper
2 Yukon Gold potatoes, sliced ¼ inch thick
    and blanched
2 leeks, cleaned, trimmed and
    coarsely chopped
2 links spicy chorizo

1 medium bulb fennel, coarsely chopped
4 sprigs fresh rosemary
4 sprigs fresh thyme
10 fresh clams
grated zest of 1 lemon
grated zest of 1 orange
2 tablespoons fresh lemon juice
2 tablespoons fresh orange juice
2 tablespoons balsamic vinegar
¼ cup extra-virgin olive oil

Preheat the oven to 375 degrees. Season the monkfish with cumin, turmeric, salt and pepper. Layer the potatoes on a 24×24-inch piece of aluminum foil. Sprinkle the leeks over the potatoes and place the fish on top of the leeks. Add the chorizo, fennel, rosemary, thyme, clams, lemon zest, orange zest, lemon juice, orange juice, vinegar and olive oil. Top with another piece of foil and seal the edges. Transfer the "hobo pack" to a baking sheet and place in the oven. Roast the fish for 35 minutes. Remove from the oven, cut open the foil and serve.

I believe that our family heritage strongly influences our feelings and attitudes about food. Growing up in America with either first- or second-generation European parents, many of us have had the privilege of inheriting their cultures, traditions, and recipes.

My family's Italian origin was an extremely strong part of my childhood. I have memories of my great-grandmother laying out her handmade pasta to dry in the house while the bouquet of aromas from her sauce filled the kitchen. Growing up in my house also meant huge Sunday dinners with more food than you can imagine. I realized early on that cooking was more than a way to feed the family; it was a comfort, an art, and a celebration of love, family, and prosperity.

peach shortcake with bourbon

serves **4**

1/4 cup (1/2 stick) butter
2 large peaches, sliced
3 ounces brown sugar
1 teaspoon chopped fresh ginger
1/4 cup bourbon
4 shortcakes, or 4 slices pound cake
1/4 cup chopped pecans
1 cup whipped cream
4 sprigs mint, for garnish

Melt the butter in a large 12-inch sauté pan over medium heat and cook until light brown. Add the peaches to the butter and sauté for 1 minute. Add the brown sugar and ginger and cook until the brown sugar melts into a caramel. Deglaze with the bourbon and cook for 1 minute.

Arrange the shortcakes or pound cake on four plates. Spoon the peaches over the cakes. Top with the chopped pecans and whipped cream. Garnish with mint sprigs.

After working in my first professional kitchen at the age of fifteen, I knew I was hooked, and I began to imagine a career that would allow me to pursue my passions in the world of food and cooking. After graduating from the Culinary Institute of America, I was fortunate enough to work with some of the greatest chefs in the world and continued to learn and grow.

Today, after cooking for more than twenty years, the spark and excitement that initially attracted me to this industry are still there. I continually challenge my knowledge and have never lost my enthusiasm. The rush that I get in the kitchen or in marketplaces on the streets in Europe is the same. When the smells are filling the kitchen, it's therapy, and it brings me right back to my childhood and the memories of stirring the sauce with my grandmother.

susan**feniger &**
marysue**milliken**

Mary Sue Milliken and Susan Feniger are two of America's most beloved chefs. The duo have been business partners for more than twenty years, beginning with the opening of City Café on Melrose Avenue in Los Angeles in 1981.

Currently, Milliken and Feniger are hands-on owner-operators of the popular and critically acclaimed Border Grill restaurants in Santa Monica and Las Vegas, serving modern Mexican food in an urban cantina setting. The pair also owns and operates Ciudad restaurant in downtown Los Angeles, featuring the bold and seductive flavors of the Latin world.

It's easy to cook really great Mexican food at home.

Natural teachers, the pair are prolific in many media. They are the authors of five cookbooks, including *Cooking with Too*

Hot Tamales, *Mesa Mexicana*, and *City Cuisine*. They are television veterans, appearing on 396 episodes of the popular *Too Hot Tamales* and *Tamales World Tour* programs on the Food Network. And they've been on the radio dial since 1996, hosting a two-hour Sunday morning talk show on KFI 640 AM in Los Angeles. In addition, Border Grill and Ciudad dishes "starred" in the 2001 Samuel Goldwyn feature film *Tortilla Soup*. Mary Sue and Susan are also the creators of the Border Girls brand of freshly prepared foods at Whole Foods Markets, as well as a line of signature pepper mills manufactured by Vic Firth. Mary Sue and Susan are active members of the community, providing leadership in many culinary associations and charities.

We got our first taste of real Mexican cooking in Chicago, circa 1978. We were working at Le Perroquet, a fine French restaurant, and watched our Latin colleagues as they prepared staff meals. They whirred up salsa in a few minutes and made rustic soups and stews with a few inexpensive ingredients. It was great, authentic cuisine that we loved to eat and so unlike the food we painstakingly prepared for the restaurant. It was quick to fix and exuberant in style, just like us. A lightbulb went off over our young heads.

Photographer &
Food Stylist
catherine**money**

basic red snapper ceviche

recipesrecipes

Basic Red Snapper Ceviche

Smoky Salsa

Shrimp and Ancho in a Bath of Garlic

Tomatillo Guacamole

Vanilla Flan

susan**feniger**
& marysue**milliken** 55

basic red snapper ceviche

Feel free to use almost any fresh fish for this crunchy raw fish salad.

serves **4 to 6**

1 pound fresh red snapper or sea bass fillets
3/4 cup freshly squeezed lime juice
1 large tomato, cored, seeded and chopped
1/2 small white onion, finely chopped
leaves of 2 bunches cilantro, coarsely chopped
4 jalapeño peppers, seeded and finely chopped
1/2 cup bottled clam juice
1 1/2 teaspoons salt
romaine lettuce leaves and tortilla chips,
   for garnish

Cut the snapper into 1/2-inch cubes and combine with 1/2 cup of the lime juice in a glass or ceramic dish. Marinate, covered, in the refrigerator for 15 minutes. Drain, discarding the lime juice.

Combine the fish with the remaining 1/4 cup lime juice and the tomato, onion, cilantro, jalapeño peppers, clam juice and salt in a medium bowl and stir to combine. Chill for at least 1 hour or up to 24 hours to blend the flavors. Serve in tall chilled goblets with spears of romaine lettuce and/or tortilla chips. You may also serve in soup bowls lined with lettuce leaves.

smoky salsa

makes **2 1/2 cups**

1 small onion, coarsely chopped
3 dried chipotle chiles, stemmed, or 1 to
   2 canned chipotle chiles, stemmed
   and rinsed
4 Roma tomatoes, cored
5 garlic cloves, peeled
1 1/2 cups water
1/2 teaspoon sugar
1 teaspoon salt
1/4 teaspoon pepper

Combine all the ingredients in a medium saucepan. Bring to a boil and reduce to a simmer. Simmer, uncovered, for 20 minutes or until the liquid is reduced by one-third and the tomato skins are falling off. Cool to room temperature. Process in a blender or food processor until smooth. Strain and chill until serving time. Store in the refrigerator for up to 5 days or freeze for up to 1 month.

It's easy to cook really great Mexican food at home. First, we want to clarify two misconceptions about cooking Mexican food. Mexican food needn't be very spicy. Once you understand how to work with chiles, recipes can easily be adjusted for the amount of heat you prefer. Certain dishes, like moles and grilled meats, are not about heat at all, but about a complex blend of flavors and sensations derived from ground vegetables, seeds and herbs, or fragrant marinades. Remember, heat can always be added at the table by serving salsas alongside, as they often do in Mexico.

shrimp and ancho in a bath of garlic

serves **4**

3/4 cup olive oil
25 garlic cloves, peeled and thinly sliced
1 3/4 pounds rock shrimp or medium shrimp,
    peeled and deveined
1 1/2 teaspoons salt
3/4 teaspoon freshly ground black pepper
3 large ancho chiles, wiped clean, stemmed,
    seeded and finely julienned
1 cup fish stock or clam juice
juice of 3 large limes
leaves of 1 bunch Italian parsley, chopped

Heat the olive oil in a large skillet over medium-low heat. Add the garlic slices and sauté until tender but not brown. Remove to a paper towel with a slotted spoon.

Toss the shrimp with the salt and pepper in a bowl. Increase the heat to high and heat until nearly smoking. Add the shrimp and sauté, stirring and shaking the skillet to prevent sticking, for 3 to 4 minutes or just until the shrimp are still slightly undercooked. Remove from the heat. Remove to a platter with a slotted spoon, reserving as many of the pan drippings in the skillet as possible.

Return the skillet to the stove and reduce the heat to medium. Return the garlic slices to the skillet and add the ancho chiles. Sauté, stirring frequently, until the oil begins to turn orange from the chiles. Stir in the fish stock along with the shrimp and any accumulated juices on the platter. Add the lime juice and parsley. Bring to a boil and remove from the heat. Serve immediately over white rice.

tomatillo guacamole

If we had to pin the essential mystery of Mexican cooking down to a single technique, it would have to be roasting and toasting. Charring foods like tomatoes, garlic, onions, and peppers and toasting seeds, spices, and grains adds that deep, smoky, rustic scent that signals authentic, soul-satisfying Mexican food—the kind you'll be making at home in no time!

To roast tomatillos, remove their husks and place in a broiler pan. Broil until totally blackened, turning and watching carefully. Remove to a bowl with any accumulated juices and add the blackened skins, which add the smoky flavor you are striving for.

makes 3 1/2 cups

1 small onion, diced
6 to 8 serrano chiles, stemmed, seeded if
    desired, and finely chopped
leaves of 1 bunch cilantro, finely chopped
1 teaspoon salt
1/2 teaspoon freshly ground pepper
12 medium tomatillos, husked, washed
    and roasted
4 large avocados, halved, seeded and peeled,
    about 2 pounds

Combine the onion, chiles, cilantro, salt and pepper in a large bowl. Add the tomatillos a few at a time, mashing and grinding with a fork or pestle to form a fine paste. Add the avocados and continue mashing and mixing until chunky. Serve with crispy fried corn chips.

Most Mexican foods are prepared with a trio of distinctly familiar ingredients: tomato, garlic, and onion. The chiles are what throw most people. If you're new to chiles, you needn't be intimidated. All you need to know is that the smaller the chile, the spicier the flavor, and that the seeds and veins inside carry the heat. So experiment accordingly. If you want chile flavor without the heat, simply remove the seeds.

vanilla flan

serves **8 to 10**

2 cups sugar
1 1/4 cups water
6 eggs
6 egg yolks
1/2 cup sugar
2 cups half-and-half
2 teaspoons vanilla extract
3 cups homemade condensed milk
1 vanilla bean

Combine 2 cups sugar with 1/2 cup of the water in a medium saucepan to make the caramel. Use a pastry brush dipped in cold water to wash the sugar crystals from the side of the saucepan. Cook over medium heat, swirling the saucepan occasionally, until the color is dark brown and the mixture has the aroma of caramel, 10 to 15 minutes. Pour enough of the mixture into a round 9-inch baking pan to coat the bottom and side, swirling to coat evenly.

Add the remaining 3/4 cup of water to the caramel remaining in the saucepan. Bring to a boil and cook over medium heat until the sugar dissolves, about 5 minutes. Stir the mixture occasionally and brush down the side of the saucepan with a pastry brush dipped in cold water to prevent crystallization. Cool to room temperature and chill until serving time.

Preheat the oven to 325 degrees. To make the flan whisk together the eggs, egg yolks, 1/2 cup sugar, half-and-half and vanilla in a large mixing bowl without incorporating air.

Pour the homemade condensed milk into a saucepan. Split the vanilla bean lengthwise and scrape the black seeds into the condensed milk with the tip of a paring knife. Add the bean and bring to a boil. Pour gradually into the egg mixture, whisking constantly. Strain into the prepared baking pan.

Place the baking pan in a larger roasting pan and add water until it reaches halfway up the side of the smaller pan. Bake for 1 hour to 1 hour and 10 minutes or until the center feels just set when pressed with your fingertips. Let cool in the water bath, then remove from the bath. Cover with plastic wrap and chill for 6 hours or longer.

To serve, run a knife around the inside edge of the pan and gently press the bottom to loosen. Cover with a platter, invert and remove the pan. Excess caramel can be drained and added to the reserved caramel sauce. Cut the flan into wedges to serve and pass the extra sauce at the table.

homemade condensed milk
6 cups nonfat milk
5 tablespoons sugar

Bring the milk to a boil in a heavy medium saucepan. Reduce to a simmer and cook for 45 minutes, stirring occasionally. Stir in the sugar and simmer for 10 to 15 minutes longer or until reduced to 3 cups; strain. Store in the refrigerator for up to a week.

gale**gand** & rick**tramonto**

Gale Gand is executive pastry chef and partner with executive chef Rick Tramonto at Tru in Chicago. Tru is an acromym for "Tramonto" and "unlimited." Tru has four stars from Mobil and was named a Relais-Gourmand property by Relais and Chateaux in 2002.

Pat Bruno of the *Chicago Sun-Times* said, "Tramonto is a blend of mad scientist and magician in the kitchen."

Rick got his start at Wendy's Old-Fashioned Hamburgers, then at the Strathallen Hotel, where he met Gale Gand. He later worked at Tavern on the Green, Gotham Bar and Grill, Aurora, Scoozi!, Avanzare, and Charlie Trotter's. He spent three years in London, transforming Stapleford Park and earning a

...a blend of mad scientist and magician

Michelin Guide Red "M" after only a year. He reopened the Criterion Brasserie in Piccadilly Circus, then returned to the United States to open Trio and Brasserie T.

Rick and Gale have written several cookbooks, including *American Brasserie*, named a finalist for the IACP Julia Child Cookbook Awards, and *Butter Sugar Flour Eggs*, nominated for a James Beard Foundation Award. Rick's latest book is *Amuse-Bouche*.

Gale started out studying silversmithing but found her true calling during a year off, when she worked in a restaurant. She started a catering company, worked at a hotel, and traveled to Europe for pastry classes and work experience. Gale's desserts were noticed by the public and restaurant reviewers alike as she worked for many well-known restaurants, including Gotham Bar and Grill, Pump Room, Bella Luna, Bice, Stapleford Park, Charlie Trotter's, Trio, Brasserie T, and, finally, Tru.

In her position as executive pastry chef, Gale has received awards from *Bon Appétit*, Robert Mondavi, *Food & Wine*, the James Beard Foundation, and the *Wine Spectator*. She has an extensive background in television broadcasting, including *Oprah* and the PBS program *Baking with Julia*.

Gale manufactures a specialty brand of root beer flavored with cinnamon, ginger, and vanilla and is a member of the culinary council for Marshall Field's.

Photographer: **toddtrice**

Food Stylist: **danmacey**

frog leg **risotto**

recipesrecipes

Frog Leg Risotto with Parsley and Lots of Garlic

Fromage Blanc Mousse

g
&
r

gale**gand**
& rick**tramonto** 61

frog leg risotto
with parsley and lots of garlic

6 cups vegetable stock

2 tablespoons unsalted butter

4 cups uncooked arborio, carnaroli or vialone nano rice

1 shallot, finely chopped

1^1/$_2$ cups white wine

1 cup chopped black trumpet mushrooms or chanterelle mushrooms

2 cups frog leg braise (page 63)

1 cup haricots verts, blanched

^{1}/$_2$ cup peeled, seeded and chopped tomato

^{1}/$_2$ cup (2 ounces) freshly grated Parmigiano-Reggiano cheese

1 cup garlic-parsley butter (page 63)

1 cup heavy cream, stiffly whipped

kosher salt and freshly ground white pepper to taste

6 frog legs, about 1 pound, for garnish (optional)

salt and pepper to taste

all-purpose flour

3 tablespoons olive oil

^{1}/$_4$ cup snipped fresh chives

grated Parmigiano-Reggiano cheese, for garnish

1 tablespoon chopped fresh tarragon, for garnish

sprigs of tarragon, for garnish

These frog legs, with all the bold garlic flavor, bring to mind classic French escargot, such as those I ate in France at Roger Vergé's restaurant, Le Moulin de Mougins, in Mougins. I co-opted those lovely flavors, substituted frogs legs for snails, worked them into a risotto—and it was magic.

As a child, there was no fear when it came to eating frog legs regularly. My Italian grandmother breaded and sautéed them in olive oil, garlic, and parsley and served them with sautéed cardoons. I lightened up the preparation here, but the spirit of the dish is true to my grandmother's. If you haven't tasted frog legs, this is a good introduction to them. And if you already share my fondness for them, you will love this. By the way, they really do taste a little like chicken!

Heat the vegetable stock in a medium saucepan over medium heat until it simmers. Reduce the heat and keep the stock at a low simmer.

Heat a large saucepan over medium heat until very hot; add the butter and let it melt. Add the rice and stir until the rice is coated with butter. Add the shallot and sauté for 3 to 4 minutes or until translucent. Add the wine and cook for 3 to 4 minutes, stirring constantly, or until the wine is reduced by half. Add the stock 1 cup at a time and cook until the rice is almost covered by the stock, stirring before the next addition. Cook for 15 minutes, stirring frequently, or until the rice is tender but still firm.

Add the mushrooms and frog leg braise meat with any liquid. Cook for 3 to 4 minutes or until heated through, stirring constantly. Add the haricots verts, tomato, cheese and garlic-parsley butter and cook until the butter melts and the vegetables are tender.

Add the whipped cream and cook until the rice is smooth and creamy. Season with salt and white pepper.

Season the frog legs with salt and pepper and dust lightly with flour. Heat the olive oil in a sauté pan over medium-high heat and add the frog legs. Cook for 1^1/2 minutes, turning several times, until golden brown. Remove to drain on paper towels.

Spoon ^{1}/2 cup of the risotto onto each serving plate and top with the chives. Garnish each with additional cheese and the chopped tarragon, 1 sprig of tarragon and top with a frog leg.

Wine: A clean, fresh, light-bodied Tocai Friulano with aromas of flowers, tropical fruit, and almonds offers textural contrast to the silky risotto and tames the assertive garlic. Ronco delle Mele from Venica and Venica in Collio, Italy, is a very fine choice with this dish.

frog leg braise

serves **4 to 6**

6 frog legs, about 1 pound
1/3 cup all-purpose flour
2 tablespoons salt
2 tablespoons freshly ground black pepper
1/4 cup olive oil
1/2 cup white wine
1/2 cup chopped carrots
1 leek, white and light green parts only,
   coarsely chopped

8 garlic cloves
2 sprigs fresh tarragon
3 sprigs fresh thyme
1 cup white wine
3/4 cup fresh lemon juice
salt and pepper to taste
4 cups chicken stock

Rinse the frog legs and pat dry. Slice the meat from the bones and reserve the bones. Mix the flour with 2 tablespoons salt and 2 tablespoons pepper. Coat the frog legs with the mixture, shaking off any excess.

Heat a large sauté pan over high heat until hot but not smoking. Reduce the heat to medium-high and add the olive oil, frog leg meat and bones. Sauté for 3 to 4 minutes, turning several times, or until golden brown. Remove and let stand until cool enough to handle. Cut the meat from the bones in chunks. Cover and refrigerate; reserve the bones.

Add 1/2 cup wine to the sauté pan and cook until the liquid has evaporated, scraping the bottom of the pan with a wooden spoon. Add the reserved bones, carrots, leek, garlic, tarragon and thyme and cook for 15 minutes, stirring occasionally, until the vegetables are tender and golden brown.

Add 1 cup wine and the lemon juice; season with salt and pepper. Cook for 8 to 10 minutes or until the liquid is reduced by 3/4. Add the chicken stock and simmer for about 1 hour or until reduced to about 1/2 cup liquid. Strain into a bowl, discarding the bones. Adjust the seasonings, add the reserved frog leg meat, and chill until needed.

garlic-parsley butter

makes **1 cup**

1 cup (2 sticks) unsalted butter,
   cut into small pieces
grated zest of 1/2 lemon
1 shallot, finely chopped
leaves of 2 bunches fresh flat-leaf parsley
cloves of 1/2 head garlic, peeled

Combine the butter, lemon zest and shallot in the bowl of a mixer fitted with a paddle attachment; beat at medium speed until smooth. Combine the parsley, garlic and 1/4 cup of the butter mixture in the bowl of a food processor fitted with a metal blade; process until smooth. Add to the mixer bowl and beat until smooth and green. Transfer to a bowl, cover with plastic wrap, and refrigerate until needed.

fromage blanc **mousse**

This is one of my favorites! If there is any category of ingredients I love to work with, it's dairy. Give me cheese, milk, yogurt, and cream any day! Essentially, this is a strawberry cheesecake made with fabulous and naturally fat-free fromage blanc, which lightens the dessert even as it enriches it. Instead of big, hulking strawberries, I use a crimson gelled distillation of the berries, which sings with full fruit flavor (although it takes hours to make). We use our strawberry "soup" or "juice" in so many ways in our kitchen. Here we gel it; in other preparations, it may be added to a sauce or used to flavor a filling.

serves **12**

3 sheets gelatin
1 pound fromage blanc
$^1/_2$ cup sugar
3 large egg yolks
$^1/_2$ cup sugar
1$^1/_2$ cups heavy cream, whipped
strawberry gelée
lemon curd paint (page 65)
blueberry stew (page 65)
lime gelée (page 65)
coconut tuiles (page 65)

Soften the gelatin in cold water in a bowl. Combine the fromage blanc and $^1/_2$ cup sugar in the top of a double boiler and place over simmering water. Cook over medium heat, stirring, until the sugar dissolves. Squeeze the water from the gelatin and add to the warm cheese mixture; whisk until the gelatin dissolves. Remove the top of the double boiler and submerge the bottom of it in an ice water bath to cool slightly and thicken the mixture.

Combine the egg yolks with $^1/_2$ cup sugar in the bowl of an electric mixer fitted with the paddle attachment. Whip at medium-high speed until thick and pale yellow. Fold into the cooled cheese mixture. Fold in the whipped cream; do not overmix.

Spoon into twelve 2$^1/_2$-inch metal rings, filling to within $^1/_4$ inch of the rim. Smooth the top and place on a sheet pan. Chill for 2 hours or until set.

Pour the hot strawberry gelée into the rings, filling to the top. Chill for 1 to 2 hours longer or until the strawberry layer is set.

To assemble, place each ring on a dessert plate. Warm the metal with a small blowtorch and lift the ring off the mousse. You may also use a hair dryer with a directed nozzle or a cloth dipped in very hot water and wrung out.

Paint a swish of lemon curd on each plate. Place a small compote of blueberry stew on the plate. Pile "rocks" of lime gelée near the mousse with a small spoon and lean a tuile against the mousse.

strawberry gelée
3 sheets gelatin
1$^1/_2$ cups strawberry juice
$^1/_4$ vanilla bean, split

Soak the gelatin in cold water in a bowl for 2 minutes to soften. Heat the strawberry juice with the vanilla bean in a small saucepan over medium heat until hot; remove from the heat. Remove the gelatin from the water and squeeze out the liquid. Add to the hot strawberry juice and stir until dissolved. Remove the vanilla bean.

garnishes for the fromage blanc mousse

serves **12**

lemon curd paint

1 cup sugar
1/2 cup (1 stick) unsalted butter
1/2 cup freshly squeezed lemon juice
1 large egg
4 large egg yolks
1/2 vanilla bean, split

Combine the sugar, butter, lemon juice, egg, egg yolks and vanilla bean in a stainless steel saucepan. Cook over medium heat, whisking constantly, for 5 to 10 minutes or until thickened; take care that the curd does not scorch.

Strain through a fine chinois or fine mesh sieve into a bowl. Cool in an ice water bath and refrigerate, covered, for up to 3 days.

blueberry stew

1 pint fresh blueberries
1 cup sugar
1/2 cup water

Combine half the blueberries, the sugar and water in a saucepan. Bring to a boil over medium-high heat. Reduce the heat and simmer for 15 minutes. Strain through a chinois or fine mesh sieve. Stir in the remaining blueberries.

lime gelée

1/2 cup water
1/4 cup freshly squeezed lime juice
1/4 cup simple syrup
3 sheets gelatin

Bring the water, lime juice and simple syrup to a boil in a saucepan over medium-high heat. Remove from the heat. Soak the gelatin in cold water in a bowl for 2 minutes. Remove from the water and squeeze gently to remove the liquid. Add to the saucepan and stir to dissolve completely. Pour into a small nonreactive container. Refrigerate, covered, until set.

coconut tuiles

1 1/4 cups sugar
2 1/2 tablespoons unsalted butter, softened
3/4 cup plus 2 tablespoons egg whites,
    from 6 or 7 large eggs
2 cups unsweetened coconut powder
1/4 cup all-purpose flour

Combine the sugar and butter in the bowl of an electric mixer fitted with the whisk attachment. Cream at medium-high speed for 2 minutes or until well mixed and sandy. Add the egg whites and mix well, scraping down the side of the bowl once or twice.

Mix the coconut powder with the flour in a small bowl. Add to the batter and mix at medium speed. Chill for 4 to 12 hours.

Preheat the oven to 300 degrees. Line a baking sheet with a Silpat. Spread 15 swatches of the batter, each 6 to 8 inches long, on the Silpat. Bake for 12 minutes or until light brown, turning halfway through the baking time.

Cool on the baking sheet and lift carefully from the sheet with a spatula. Store in an airtight container.

To make coconut powder for the tuiles, chop fresh coconut into small pieces and process until powdery in a food processor fitted with a metal blade, or process unsweetened coconut flakes to a powder.

gale**gand**
& rick**tramonto** 65

chris**hastings**

Christopher Hastings is co-owner and executive chef of the Hot and Hot Fish Club in Birmingham, Alabama. The forty-one-year-old native of Charlotte, North Carolina, and graduate of Johnson and Wales, was a 1998 recipient of the Robert Mondavi Culinary Award of Excellence for Best Restaurant.

In 1989, Hastings worked with Bradley Ogden to open the Lark Creek Inn in San Francisco. Working as sous chef gave Hastings the opportunity to discover his own style, and he credits Ogden for his tremendous influence: "Brad's unrelenting pursuit of intense, clear flavor was never compromised. He also opened my eyes to the local farmer and how he could impact the food and help set it apart from the others."

In 1995, Hastings returned to the South and opened the Hot and Hot Fish Club with his wife, Idie, who serves as general manager. The restaurant is located in a historic building on Birmingham's southside and has earned a reputation for serving some of the finest, freshest dishes in the region. He was voted Birmingham's Best Chef in *Birmingham Magazine*'s 2000 and 2001 readers' poll. Hastings developed his love for and relationship with food during family vacations spent in the low country of South Carolina.

...the basic mission— to make people happy with great food

My particular journey to becoming a chef began in my childhood, spending all my summers in the low country of South Carolina at Pawley's Island. There, I learned to be the creek boy for our family, providing what the salt marsh had to offer: crabs, shrimp, oysters, clams, and a variety of great fish that my mother and aunts would serve up with fresh, seasonal vegetables. I learned the long and rich history of my family and the importance of being at the table with family and friends, the bonds formed, and the power of the dining experience. These times taught me who I am and what is at the heart of my career as a chef. I am passionate about my family and the outdoors and the products it provides. The profound experience of dining with close friends and family, while leaving all the worries and pretenses of the day behind, exemplifies the Hot and Hot Fish Club's basic mission.

Photographer
corinnecolen

Food Stylist
delorescuster

seared **gulf snapper**

recipesrecipes

Seared Gulf Snapper with Garden Winter Vegetables and Lemon Caper Sauce

Hot and Hot Tomato Salad

chris**hastings** 67

seared gulf snapper
with garden winter vegetables and lemon caper sauce

serves 4

4 (6-ounce) red snapper fillets
salt and pepper to taste
1/4 cup peanut oil or vegetable oil
1/4 cup (1/2 stick) butter
1 small shallot, minced
chopped fresh thyme to taste
4 whole chioga or golden beets, roasted,
　　peeled and split
4 baby fennel, blanched and split
4 red baby carrots, blanched and peeled
　　with 1/4 inch stem on
4 white baby carrots, blanched and peeled
　　with 1/4 inch stem on
4 purple fingerling potatoes, cooked and split
4 yellow turnips, blanched and split
　　with 1/4 inch stem on
4 cipollini onions, roasted and peeled
8 haricots verts, blanched
lemon caper sauce
4 teaspoons bias-cut chives

Season the red snapper with salt and pepper. Coat a heavy skillet with the peanut oil and heat over high heat until it begins to smoke. Add the fish skin side down and cook until golden brown and crispy on the skin side. Flip and place in a 400-degree oven for 4 minutes. Remove and hold warm.

Heat the butter in a large heavy-bottomed sauté pan over medium heat. Add the shallot and thyme and cook for 2 minutes. Add the beets, fennel, carrots, potatoes, turnips and onions. Toss together, coating well. Season with salt and pepper. Place in a 400-degree oven and bake for 10 minutes. Add the haricots verts and cook 3 minutes longer.

Arrange the vegetables on 4 plates. Place the fish on the vegetables and spoon the sauce over and around the fish. Sprinkle with the chives. Serve immediately.

lemon caper sauce
2 shallots, minced
1/2 cup white wine
1/4 cup white wine vinegar
2 sprigs fresh thyme
3/4 cup (1 1/2 sticks) butter
2 tablespoons lemon juice
2 ounces capers

Combine the shallots, wine, vinegar and thyme in a heavy saucepot. Cook over low heat until reduced by 90 percent. Whisk in the butter, making sure not to boil and break the sauce. When all the butter is incorporated, remove from the heat. Add the lemon juice and capers. Hold for up to 30 minutes in a warm spot.

hot and hot tomato salad

serves 6

6 large beefsteak tomatoes, sliced
2 large golden delight tomatoes, sliced
2 big rainbow tomatoes, sliced
balsamic vinaigrette
salt and pepper to taste
4 ounces fresh butter beans
½ small onion, chopped
1 teaspoon fresh thyme
bacon trimmings
kernels of 3 ears of queen corn, cooked
½ pint sweet 100 tomatoes
fried okra
4 thin slices applewood smoked bacon,
    cooked until crisp
chive aïoli

Toss the sliced tomatoes in the balsamic vinaigrette in a bowl. Season with salt and pepper. Set aside.

Simmer the butter beans with the onion, thyme, bacon trimmings and salt in enough water to cover in a saucepan until just tender. Cool and set aside in a small bowl. Combine the corn kernels with some of the balsamic vinaigrette in a bowl and let stand.

To assemble, arrange the sliced tomatoes on plates. Place whole sweet 100 tomatoes around the sliced tomatoes. Divide the butter beans and corn mixture evenly among the plates. Arrange fried okra and the bacon on the plates. Drizzle the chive aïoli over all and serve.

balsamic vinaigrette

½ cup extra-virgin olive oil
½ cup pure olive oil
1 cup picked basil leaves, thinly sliced
½ cup sliced scallions
1 cup balsamic vinegar
salt and pepper to taste

Combine the olive oils, basil, scallions and balsamic vinegar in a bowl and mix well. Season with salt and pepper. Hold until needed.

chive aïoli

2 large garlic cloves, finely minced
1 medium bunch chives, thinly sliced
1 egg yolk
juice of 1 small lemon
salt and pepper to taste
1 cup olive oil
¼ cup crème fraîche

Combine the garlic and chives in a small bowl. Add the egg yolk, lemon juice, salt and pepper. Whisk in the olive oil vigorously, being sure to create an emulsion. Add the crème fraîche. Add a drop or two of water if too thick.

karen**hilliard**

Much of Karen Hilliard's youth was spent in food meccas such as Chicago, New Orleans, and the suburbs of New York City. But it wasn't until she was a housewife in West Texas that she realized she was an artist and food was her medium.

Today, Karen is co-founder and co-owner of Atlanta's successful Georgia Grille, a unique situation that brings her back full circle to the city where she was born. Her foray into food began with a catering company in Texas, a cooking school, and a stint on the local NBC affiliate. She studied with Francois Dionot at the Bethesda L'Academie des Cuisine and Nathalie Dupree at Rich's Cooking School in Atlanta. Hilliard also studied at La Varenne in Paris, France.

...flavors of the Southwest blended with Southern tastes and French techniques

In 1983, she opened Peach's in Odessa, Texas, featuring American cuisine with a Southern attitude. The experience honed her skills as a food artist and entrepreneur, and she opened a second restaurant, Karen's, atop Midland's Bank Building.

In 1989, she and her son, Billy Kennedy, moved to Atlanta to open Georgia Grille, a neighborhood bistro featuring southwestern comfort food. "As with life, a restaurant is about growth and change," says Hilliard. "Both are built upon layers of experience, taste, and people. The unique flavors at Georgia Grille are the result of blending those layers." Five years later, their success spawned a second location, Toulouse, which emphasizes New American cuisine. Toulouse is noted both for its food and its dramatic interior, conceived by Hilliard, who studied restaurant design at Harvard. Hilliard has since sold Toulouse to concentrate on Georgia Grille.

In 1994, Hilliard self-published a cookbook, *Teaching Billy to Cook*, which chronicles her recipes and budding business partner-ship with her thirty-something son. It was illustrated by her late husband, John Ehrlichman.

Photographer
dawnsmith

Food Stylist
nancymeyer

grilled **pork chops**

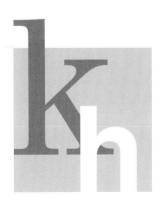

recipesrecipes

Grilled Pork Chops with Peach Bourbon Chutney and Fried Collard Greens

Key Lime Margarita

Breakfast Eggs with Corn Tortillas and Chile Sauce

Triple Chocolate Mousse

Kahlúa Chocolate Crème Brûlée

karenhilliard 71

grilled pork chops with peach bourbon chutney and fried collard greens

serves 6

6 very thick pork chops
vegetable oil
salt and pepper to taste
creamy jalapeño cheese grits
peach bourbon chutney
fried collard greens

Brush the pork chops with oil and sprinkle lightly with salt and pepper. Place on a heated grill and grill until cooked through.

Spoon the creamy jalapeño grits onto 6 serving plates and place 1 pork chop on each plate. Top with the peach bourbon chutney and fried collard greens.

creamy jalapeño cheese grits
1 cup quick-cooking grits
2 cups milk
1 cup heavy cream
2 cups water
1 egg
1 cup (4 ounces) shredded
  Monterey Jack cheese
2 tablespoons butter
1 jalapeño pepper, roasted and chopped
  (seeds optional)
2 teaspoons salt

Soak the grits in the milk and cream in a bowl for as long as possible. Heat the water to a boil in a saucepan and stir in the grits mixture. Bring to a boil and reduce the heat. Cook until slightly thickened. Stir in the egg, cheese, butter, jalapeño pepper and salt.

Pour into a baking dish and bake at 350 degrees for 20 minutes. The grits should be creamy; add additional milk or cream if they are dry. Adjust the seasoning.

peach bourbon chutney
1 teaspoon minced garlic
1 teaspoon minced shallot
1/2 teaspoon minced jalapeño pepper
2 teaspoons vegetable oil
1 cup apple cider vinegar
1/2 cup sugar
1/2 cup packed brown sugar
3 cups chopped peeled fresh or frozen peaches
1/2 teaspoon ground cloves
1/2 teaspoon red chili powder
1/2 teaspoon dry mustard
1/2 cup bourbon

Sauté the garlic, shallot and jalapeño pepper in the oil in a nonreactive saucepan for about 1 minute. Stir in the vinegar, sugar and brown sugar and bring to a boil slowly, stirring occasionally and making sure that the sugars are melted before boiling. Reduce the heat to medium and add the peaches, cloves, chili powder, dry mustard and bourbon. Serve warm with grilled pork chops or other grilled meat or chicken. You may process in a food processor for a smoother consistency if preferred.

fried collard greens
1 pound fresh collard greens, trimmed
vegetable oil for frying

Wash the collard greens in several changes of water. Roll several leaves at a time into a cigar shape and cut into 1-inch chiffonade strips. Heat oil to 360 degrees in a very deep fryer. Add the collard greens in small batches; they will bubble and spatter in the oil. Deep-fry for 15 seconds or until the spatter slows; remove and drain on thick paper towels to absorb the oil. Serve immediately or keep crisp until needed.

key lime margarita

serves **1**

lime juice
salt
1½ ounces (3 tablespoons) Gold Tequila
½ ounce (1 tablespoon) Cointreau
key lime/simple syrup mix

key lime/simple syrup mix
sugar
water
2½ cups Key lime juice
¼ cup orange juice

Swirl the rim of a 10- or 12-ounce glass in lime juice, dip in salt and fill with crushed ice. Combine the tequila, Cointreau and key lime/simple syrup mix in a shaker filled with ice. Shake to mix well and strain into the prepared glass.

Prepare a Mexican Margarita in the same manner, using 2½ ounces Silver Tequila, 1½ ounces Triple Sec and fresh lime juice.

Combine 2 parts sugar to 1 part water in a saucepan and bring to a boil slowly, stirring to dissolve the sugar completely.

Combine 1½ cups of the simple syrup with the Key lime juice and orange juice in a pitcher and mix well.

As I was perfecting my culinary skills in Atlanta, Chicago, New Orleans, West Texas, New Mexico, and France, I did not suspect that the path would bring me back to where it all began. Looking back at all the gaining and losing, marriage, children, and other enterprises, I can't imagine it happening any other way. I brought only the essentials with me in 1990 when I left West Texas—an old Coca-Cola cooler, an equally aged oven, a lot of memories, and many dreams. As I made my home once again in Atlanta, the cooler and the oven found honored places at Georgia Grille. In many ways, our journey was just beginning then. Ahead, the challenge of teaching my son, Billy, to cook would become the most important and necessary part of our success.

breakfast eggs
with corn tortillas and chile sauce

serves 6

2 pounds plum tomatoes
3 New Mexico green chiles
2 garlic cloves, unpeeled
1/2 cup chopped onion
1 tablespoon vegetable oil
1 tablespoon cider vinegar
1 1/2 teaspoons sugar
1/2 teaspoon ground cumin
1/8 teaspoon dried oregano
1 1/2 tablespoons lime juice
salt to taste
vegetable oil for frying
6 corn tortillas
6 eggs
shredded Cheddar cheese

Place the tomatoes, chiles and garlic in a broiler pan. Broil until the skins blister and blacken, turning frequently. Cool, peel and chop the tomatoes. Seed and chop the chiles; mince the garlic.

Sauté the onion in 1 tablespoon oil in a saucepan over medium heat. Add the roasted vegetables, vinegar, sugar, cumin and oregano; simmer for 3 to 4 minutes. Stir in the lime juice and season with salt. Simmer for several minutes.

Pour oil to a depth of 1 inch in a skillet and heat over high heat. Add the tortillas 1 at a time and fry until crisp but not "crackable." Pour off all but a film of oil and fry the eggs until done to taste.

Place 1 tortilla on each plate and spoon the tomato-chile sauce over the tortillas. Add 1 egg to each plate and top with a sprinkle of cheese. Serve immediately.

The depth of taste and flavor that comes from smoking and roasting can be subtle or intense. Either way, it is addictive. When I discovered this magic, it opened up a flood of ideas that have become award-winning dishes! At the same time, another kind of magic was going on at Georgia Grille. As the days passed, Billy mastered the basics of cooking, and we began to have time to experiment. We gained confidence in each other, in ourselves, and in our ability to serve wonderful food to our customers. We finally relaxed, really happy with what we were doing, and our little restaurant became a success.

triple chocolate mousse

12 ounces bittersweet chocolate
1/2 cup sugar
1/2 cup strong hot coffee
4 egg yolks
1 tablespoon dark rum or vanilla extract
4 egg whites
pinch of salt

1/4 teaspoon cream of tartar
3/4 cup sugar
3 cups heavy cream
1/2 cup crushed chocolate wafers
2 ounces bittersweet chocolate, shaved
1/2 cup whipped cream, for garnish
1/2 cup warmed fudge sauce, for garnish

Process 12 ounces bittersweet chocolate to fine granules in a food processor. Add 1/2 cup sugar and the hot coffee, processing constantly. Add the egg yolks 1 at a time, processing until smooth after each addition. Add the rum.

Beat the egg whites with the salt in a large bowl until foamy. Add the cream of tartar and beat until peaks begin to form. Add 3/4 cup sugar gradually, beating until moderately stiff.

Whip 3 cups cream in a bowl until soft peaks form. Fold the whipped cream and then the egg whites into the chocolate mixture. Stir in the cookie crumbs and shaved chocolate.

Pour into a serving container and freeze until firm. Let stand at room temperature for 1 hour before serving. Garnish with 1/2 cup whipped cream and the fudge sauce.

kahlúa chocolate crème brûlée

serves **6**

3 cups heavy cream
1/4 cup chopped chocolate
2/3 cup sugar
6 egg yolks
1/4 cup Kahlúa

Preheat the oven to 350 degrees. Heat the heavy cream to a simmer in a saucepan and stir in the chocolate until melted. Combine the sugar, egg yolks and Kahlúa in a separate bowl, mixing well. Add the chocolate mixture.

Pour into ramekins. Place the ramekins in a baking dish deep enough to hold 1 inch of water. Add hot water to the baking dish. Bake for 20 to 30 minutes.

louise**lamensdorf**

Louise Lamensdorf has spent the past twenty-five years creating her own style of cuisine. This Louisiana native with a French grandmother fell in love with French food at an early age.

In 1979, Louise opened the French Apron School of Cooking in Fort Worth, Texas. During the ten years the school operated, she apprenticed regularly with world-acclaimed Hall of Fame Master Chef Charles Finance. Louise also apprenticed at Michelin-starred French restaurants in southwestern France and on the Riviera, played host to prominent, well-established chefs, such as Stephan Pyles and Madeleine Kamman, and became a principal teacher of world cuisines.

Louise has served as executive chef at award-winning restaurants in Fort Worth since 1988. In 1996, she opened Bistro Louise to serve her innovative and individualistic Mediterranean cuisine. Bistro Louise has earned awards galore, including top *Zagat* ratings for food and popularity, *Gourmet*'s Top Tables, and many local awards for Best French Restaurant.

...*innovative and individualistic Mediterranean cuisine*

Additional training with Jacques Pépin, the Cordon Bleu in New York, and, more recently, Michelin-starred chef Jacques Chibois in Grasse, France, and Don Alfonso in St. Agatha, Italy, keeps Louise on the cutting edge of modern Mediterranean cuisine.

Photographer
mike**rutherford**

Food Stylist
maryanne**fowlkes**

citrus **soufflé tart**

recipesrecipes

Citrus Soufflé Tart

San Francisco Cioppino

Salmon on a Bed of Herbed Risotto

Chocolate Fig Steamed Pudding

louise**lamensdorf** 77

citrus soufflé tart

serves **10**

5 egg yolks
6 tablespoons sugar
1/4 cup lime juice
1/4 cup grapefruit juice
1/4 cup orange juice
1/4 cup passion fruit concentrate
1/4 cup (1/2 stick) unsalted butter,
    at room temperature
4 egg whites
1/8 teaspoon salt
1/2 cup sugar
citrus crust
confectioners' sugar, for garnish
citrus sauce

Beat the egg yolks in a bowl until foamy. Add 6 tablespoons sugar and beat until the mixture forms a ribbon. Stir in the lime juice, grapefruit juice, orange juice and passion fruit concentrate. Pour the mixture into a saucepan and whisk in the butter. Cook over low heat, stirring constantly, until the mixture thickens. Pour into a bowl and refrigerate until the mixture is firm, about 3 hours.

Beat the egg whites with the salt until peaks begin to form. Add 1/2 cup sugar gradually and beat until the egg whites are firm and shiny. Stir 1/4 of the egg white mixture into the soufflé filling to lighten the mixture. Fold in the remaining egg white mixture gently.

Pour into the baked tart shell. Bake for 15 minutes in an oven preheated to 375 degrees.

Cool for 1 hour. Garnish with confectioners' sugar. Serve with citrus sauce prepared by making another soufflé filling and adding 1/2 cup whipped cream instead of the egg whites and sugar.

citrus crust

2 1/4 cups unbleached all-purpose flour
2 tablespoons sugar
grated zest of 1 orange
1/8 teaspoon salt
3/4 cup (1 1/2 sticks) unsalted butter,
    diced and frozen
2 tablespoons Cointreau

Process the flour, sugar, orange zest and salt in a food processor until the orange zest is well combined. Add the butter and pulse until the mixture becomes the consistency of a coarse meal. Add the Cointreau through the feed tube in a steady stream, processing constantly until the dough begins to form a ball.

Shape into a circle and refrigerate for at least 1 hour. Roll the dough to fit an 11-inch tart pan. Chill for at least 1 hour. Bake at 350 to 375 degrees for 20 minutes; cool.

san francisco cioppino

serves **6**

1/2 cup olive oil

1 small onion, chopped

leaves of 1 large sprig rosemary, coarsely chopped, about 1/4 cup

2 bay leaves

2 large carrots, julienned

1 leek, finely sliced

18 mussels, washed and cleaned

12 clams, washed

2 mushrooms, preferably shiitake, thinly sliced

1 green bell pepper, chopped

2 garlic cloves, crushed and finely chopped

1 small bunch parsley with stems, chopped

1 tomato, peeled and chopped

6 to 12 shrimp, peeled

2 lobster tails (optional)

1/2 cup dry vermouth

1 cup white wine

1 chicken bouillon cube

6 cups water

1/4 cup tomato paste

1 rib celery, thinly sliced on the diagonal

6 to 8 breakfast radishes, thinly sliced

1 teaspoon salt

1/2 teaspoon black pepper

1 teaspoon soy sauce

8 to 10 drops Tabasco sauce

few strands saffron

oysters (optional)

6 basil leaves, chopped

Heat the olive oil in a nonstick, nonmetallic saucepan. Add the onion and sauté until glazed. Add the rosemary, bay leaves, carrots, leek, mussels, clams, mushrooms and bell pepper. Sauté over medium heat until the mussels and clams open and the vegetables are al dente.

Add the garlic, parsley and tomato. Sauté for 1 to 2 minutes. Add the shrimp and lobster. Sauté until well incorporated with the vegetables.

Add the vermouth to the saucepan, stirring to deglaze. Cook until slightly reduced. Add the wine and cook until slightly reduced.

Mix the chicken bouillon cube with the water and tomato paste in a bowl. Add to the vegetable and seafood mixture and bring to a boil. Add the celery and radishes. Season with the salt, pepper, soy sauce, Tabasco sauce and saffron.

Simmer for 10 to 15 minutes. Add the oysters and finish just before serving by adding the basil. Taste for salt and pepper. Serve immediately.

salmon on a bed of herbed risotto

serves 6

6 salmon fillet portions, trimmed and deboned
all-purpose flour
herbed risotto
syrah syrup (optional)

Dust the salmon lightly with flour on one side, shaking off the excess. Sear the salmon flour side down in a hot sauté pan until caramelized. Turn the salmon and cook to the desired doneness. Finish on top of the stove or in the oven.

Spoon the herbed risotto into the center of each serving plate. Top with the salmon. Circle with syrah syrup if desired.

herbed risotto

1 cup fresh spinach
2 tablespoons olive oil
3/4 cup mixture of leaves of fresh rosemary,
    thyme, marjoram and basil, very finely
    chopped
grated zest of 1 lemon
4 1/2 to 5 cups chicken stock
3 to 4 tablespoons olive oil
2 cups finely chopped onions
2 cups uncooked arborio rice
1 cup uncooked white rice
white wine
freshly grated Parmesan cheese
butter
salt and pepper to taste

Purée the spinach with 2 tablespoons olive oil in a food processor; you should have 1/2 cup purée. Combine with the herb mixture and lemon zest to form a paste. Set aside.

Bring the chicken stock to a simmer in a saucepan and hold at a low simmer.

Preheat a saucepan. Add 3 to 4 tablespoons olive oil. Add the onions and sauté until wilted but not brown. Add the rice and sauté, stirring just until the rice is coated and well heated. Deglaze the saucepan with wine. Reduce the heat and cook until all of the wine is absorbed by the rice.

Add 1 1/2 cups of the simmering chicken stock to the rice. Cook, rotating the saucepan over low to medium heat, until all the liquid is absorbed. Add the remaining stock 1 cup at a time and cook after each addition until the stock is well absorbed. This whole process should take approximately 20 minutes.

Stir in the desired amount of the herb purée and heat to serving temperature. Finish with Parmesan cheese and butter. Season with salt and pepper.

Note: You may prepare the risotto up to 24 hours in advance and spread on a sheet pan covered with parchment paper to cool. Combine the risotto and herb mixture in a sauté pan at serving time. Add 1/2 cup additional hot stock and cook until the risotto becomes hot and creamy again.

chocolate fig steamed pudding

serves **8**

1 cup all-purpose flour
¹/2 teaspoon salt
2 teaspoons baking powder
¹/4 cup baking cocoa
³/4 cup milk
¹/4 cup Frangelico
1 cup puréed canned, dried or fresh figs or
   a combination

¹/2 cup (1 stick) butter, softened
1 cup sugar
3 eggs
4 ounces European bittersweet chocolate,
   finely chopped
1 cup finely chopped walnuts

Mix together the flour, salt, baking powder and cocoa. Mix together the milk, Frangelico and figs in a bowl.

Cream the butter and sugar in a mixing bowl until light. Beat in the eggs. Alternate adding the dry ingredients and milk mixture to the creamed mixture and mixing at low speed until well combined. Fold in the chocolate and walnuts quickly.

Spoon into a buttered 5-cup steamed pudding mold, filling almost full. Cover with heavy-duty foil. Place in a larger pan with water reaching halfway up the side of the mold.

Bring the water to a boil, then reduce the heat slightly to a gentle simmer. Cover the larger pan and mold with foil. Cook at a gentle simmer for 1¹/2 to 2 hours or until the top of the pudding is set and dry. Remove the mold from the water and let stand for 2 to 3 minutes. Invert onto parchment paper. Serve with hot fudge sauce and fresh California Black Mission figs or large Mediterranean figs.

You can prepare the pudding a day ahead and store it in the refrigerator. Reheat in the microwave for 1¹/2 minutes.

jenifer**lang**

Since 1990, Jenifer has been managing director of the three-star Café des Artistes in New York City, a restaurant frequently cited as one of the best in the United States and always on the top twenty in the _Zagat Survey_.

Jenifer Lang has combined a love for words and food into a career that's part cooking and part publishing. It is a road colored by experiences in the kitchen of her Jewish grandmother, who was married to an Irish Catholic. She trained at the Culinary Institute of America, then worked in the kitchen of New York's 21 Club restaurant, the first woman to do so. She became the chef at Nathan's in Georgetown while writing a column for the _Washington Post_ entitled "The Resolute Shopper." That column turned into a book, _Tastings: The Best from Ketchup to Caviar_, which received the prestigious Tastemaker award. It was revised and republished in 1996 as _The Best of Kitchen Basics_.

United Airlines passengers in the 1980s probably read Jenifer's work: she wrote two columns, "Tastings" and "The Picnic Basket,"

for the airline's monthly magazine between 1984 and 1989. Around the same time, she edited a food newsletter entitled _Great Taste: The Food Discovery Newsletter_ and wrote a column for _European Travel and Life_ magazine entitled "Foreign Affairs."

Jenifer also was the American editor for the 1988 edition of _Larousse Gastronimique_, the encyclopedia of French cuisine. Her recipes and her articles on food, restaurants, and consumer subjects appear frequently in national food and general interest magazines.

She authored a children's cookbook, _Jenifer Lang Cooks for Kids: 153 Recipes and Ideas for Good Food That Kids Love to Eat_. In 1992, Doubleday asked Jenifer to create an imprint within the publishing house, which was dubbed Jenifer Lang/Doubleday Publishers.

traditional bûche de noël

Photographer
mike**rutherford**

Food Stylist
maryanne**fowlkes**

Romance and love of good food can overcome seemingly improbable marriages.

recipesrecipes

Traditional Bûche de Noël

Mimi's Sauerkraut Cooked with Apples

Boppa's Giblet Gravy

jenifer**lang** 83

traditional **bûche de noël**

serves **12**

4 egg yolks

2/3 cup sugar

1 cup cake flour, sifted

grated zest of 1 orange

1 teaspoon baking powder

pinch of salt

1 teaspoon vanilla extract

4 egg whites

pinch of cream of tartar

1/3 cup sugar

confectioners' sugar in
  a shaker

chocolate filling and frosting

meringue mushrooms
  (page 85)

3 tablespoons unsweetened
  baking cocoa

The symbolism of the bûche de Noël dates back to the ancient Celtic tradition of celebrating the winter solstice, when a large log was burned as a symbol of the rebirth of the sun. It later became a small branch used as a centerpiece surrounded by sweets and, finally, the sweet itself—the cake that we know today. I serve it during the holiday season at my Café des Artistes on Central Park West. Vladimir Horowitz loved it so much that he would run his finger along the edge of the cake display on the way to his table while his wife, Wanda, slapped his offending hand.

Preheat the oven to 375 degrees. Place the oven rack in the center of the oven. Grease the bottom of a 10×15-inch jelly roll pan and line with parchment paper.

Whip the egg yolks with 2/3 cup sugar in the bowl of an electric mixer until thick and pale yellow. Add the flour, orange zest, baking powder, salt and vanilla gradually, mixing constantly until all are incorporated.

Whip the egg whites in a mixer bowl until they are foamy. Sprinkle the cream of tartar over the whites and continue to whip until they form soft peaks.

Add 1/3 cup sugar to the egg whites 1 teaspoon at a time, beating until it is all incorporated and the whites are shiny and stiff. Stir 1/4 of the whipped egg whites into the yolk mixture and then gently fold in the remaining egg whites.

Spoon the batter into the prepared jelly roll pan and smooth the top carefully with a spatula. Tap the pan gently on the table to remove any air bubbles in the batter. Bake for approximately 8 to 10 minutes, or until the cake is light golden and springs back when lightly touched. Remove from the oven and immediately sprinkle the cake liberally with confectioners' sugar. Cut around the edges to free the cake from the pan.

Cover the cake with a dry and clean kitchen towel and roll up the cake the long way, rolling the towel inside the cake as you go. Let cool completely.

Unroll the cake and trim about 1/4 inch off all sides to help with the rolling. Spread the chocolate filling over the entire surface of the cake. Roll the cake tightly to enclose the filling. Slice off a narrow piece on the bias from each end. Place the log seam side down on a serving platter and place one of the ends on the top of the log to simulate a cut branch.

Frost the entire log with chocolate frosting and drag the tines of a fork across the surface to resemble lines on the bark of a tree, adding a knot or two, if you like! Dust with additional confectioners' sugar to simulate snow. Arrange the mushrooms in little clusters on and around the log. Sprinkle them lightly with the baking cocoa.

chocolate filling and frosting

2 teaspoons instant coffee granules
3 tablespoons dark rum
12 ounces bittersweet chocolate, melted
1/2 cup (1 stick) unsalted butter, at room
  temperature
reserved meringue mixture (page 85)

Dissolve the instant coffee granules in the rum in a cup. Combine the melted chocolate, rum mixture and half the softened butter with the reserved meringue mixture; beat until smooth. Remove 2/3 of this mixture from the bowl and reserve for the frosting. Beat the remaining butter into the chocolate mixture remaining in the bowl for the filling.

meringue mushrooms

The meringue used to create the meringue mushrooms is also used for the chocolate filling and frosting for the traditional bûche de Noël.

serves **12**

3 egg whites
pinch of salt
¹/₄ teaspoon cream of tartar
1 cup sugar

Whip the egg whites in a bowl until foamy. Sprinkle the salt and cream of tartar over the whites and continue whipping at low speed. At the same time, combine the sugar with enough water to resemble wet sand in a small saucepan. Cook over medium-high heat until the mixture boils and reaches 238 degrees, soft-ball stage, on a candy thermometer.

Increase the speed of the mixer that is whipping the whites and continue until they form soft peaks. Drizzle the hot sugar mixture gradually into the whites, whipping constantly until the whites are at room temperature; they should be thick and shiny.

Preheat the oven to 200 degrees. Line the bottom of a 10×15-inch jelly roll pan with parchment paper. Fit a round tip onto a pastry bag and fill with ¹/₄ of the meringue mixture. Reserve the remainder of the meringue for the filling and frosting. Pipe about twelve ¹/₂-inch mounds onto the prepared jelly roll pan to resemble mushroom caps. Then pipe out the same amount of cone-shaped stems onto the same pan.

Bake approximately 1¹/₂ to 2 hours, or until the meringues look set. Remove from the oven and let cool; they will stiffen up. Glue the caps to the stems with a little frosting.

Having a quirky family can be trying; one thing you can say—it's never dull. Mine was full of drama and intrigue, laced with a certain schizophrenia. Take my paternal grandparents, for instance: my grandmother was an Orthodox Jew and my grandfather a superstitious Irish Catholic. This lifelong love affair between two strong-willed people produced profound cultural and religious influences in my childhood. As a result, we accepted these two wildly different ways of thinking quite comfortably. We dutifully went to the local Catholic church every Sunday with Boppa, learning the Baltimore catechism and the Latin Mass— and invariably behaving so disgracefully during the service that the priest regularly ended his sermon with, ". . . and the Lonergan children must come to see me in the rectory directly after Mass!" As a neat balancing act, we learned from my grandmother to light candles every Friday night, as her family had done since time immemorial. We all learned a great deal of Yiddish, which was my grandmother's first language; little did I know that it would come in quite handy when I moved to New York.

mimi's sauerkraut cooked with apples

serves **8**

3 slices bacon, diced

3/4 cup chopped onion

4 cups drained sauerkraut (about 2 pounds
    undrained), either made from scratch
    or packaged

1 1/4 cups (1/2-inch) pieces apple

1 1/2 cups Champagne or white wine

10 juniper berries, in a tea ball or a piece
    of cheesecloth

boppa's giblet gravy (page 87)

Sauté the bacon with the onion in a heavy nonaluminum saucepan over medium heat, stirring frequently, for about 15 minutes, or until the onion is translucent.

Add the sauerkraut, apple, Champagne and juniper berries and partially cover the saucepan. Adjust the heat so that the liquid simmers and cook for 40 minutes, stirring occasionally. Discard the juniper berries and serve the sauerkraut in a covered vegetable dish with boppa's giblet gravy.

boppa's giblet gravy

No one in my family can tell me how or when someone first decided to put the giblet gravy on top of the sauerkraut as well as the mashed potatoes at our Christmas dinners, but we are forever grateful for the original audacity. Our spouses hear many stories about the larger-than-life patriarch and matriarch of the Lonergan clan, and I'm sure most of them are sick of the anecdotes. No doubt it's just easier to take the sauerkraut with giblet gravy, which lives on from year to year on all of our Christmas tables, deliciously proving that romance and love of good food can overcome seemingly improbable marriages.

serves 8

1 medium unpeeled onion
1 pound chicken or turkey giblets, rinsed
    and drained (see note)
2 cups chopped celery
2 cups chopped carrots
1 cup chopped unpeeled onion
4 cups chicken broth
1 teaspoon whole black peppercorns
5 whole cloves
1 bay leaf
$^1/_2$ cup roasted turkey drippings, or $^1/_2$ cup
    (1 stick) unsalted butter
$^1/_2$ cup all-purpose flour
salt and freshly ground pepper to taste

Heat a heavy skillet over high heat for 3 minutes. Cut the whole onion into halves and place cut side down in the hot skillet. Cook until the cut surfaces are completely blackened, about 3 to 5 minutes. Place the charred onion in a heavy stockpot and add the giblets, celery, carrots, chopped onion, chicken broth, peppercorns, cloves, bay leaf and 4 cups water. Bring to a boil and stir. Reduce the heat so that the stock simmers slowly. Cook, uncovered, for 2 hours, stirring once or twice. Pour the stock through a strainer and reserve 4 cups stock. Cool the solid ingredients enough to handle, remove the giblets and reserve. Discard the remaining vegetables and seasonings.

Heat the turkey drippings in a heavy medium saucepan over medium heat and stir in the flour. Cook, stirring constantly, until the mixture has turned a golden brown color, about 5 minutes. Pour in the hot stock and whisk while bringing to a boil. Add salt and pepper. Reduce the heat to a slow simmer and cook the gravy, uncovered, stirring occasionally, for 15 minutes.

Chop the giblets into very small pieces, about $^1/_8$- to $^1/_4$-inch dice, in a food processor or by hand. Add to the gravy and heat for 2 more minutes. Serve in a gravy boat at the table, to be used on turkey, mashed potatoes and especially the sauerkraut.

Note: You can collect poultry giblets—gizzards and hearts, but no livers—in the freezer and defrost them for this recipe, or buy the whole lot from a butcher.

One side benefit of my grandparentage was that we all got to celebrate twice as many holidays as anyone else. Included in the festivities was a massive Christmas dinner that was Norman Rockwellian in its American correctness. The one oddity in this feast was that served at dinner right alongside everything else, in an ornate sterling silver Victorian vegetable dish, was a somewhat unusual family specialty: sauerkraut with giblet gravy. It never seemed unusual to me, of course. It was always my favorite part of the dinner.

edwardlee

It seems like destiny, not an accident, that this Brooklyn, New York, native found his way to Louisville, Kentucky, and made a home there. He says, "When you get to know me, you quickly learn that I am a country boy at heart."

Chef Edward Lee was only thirty-one when he found 610 Magnolia in the heart of old Louisville. He was so impressed with the restaurant and local farms and artisans upon his first visit during Derby Week that he returned two years later to make the place his own. Lee shares many culinary and agricultural philosophies with former owner Ed Garber, believing that " . . . every meal is a narrative. To cook a meal is to tell a story using the ingredients as a vocabulary. That is why I prepare multi-course meals, because it is the only way to complete the narrative."

Having graduated with a magna cum laude degree in literature from New York University, it's only fitting that Lee uses a literary analogy to describe his culinary philosophy.

He spent much of his life in New York and believes that the urban life played a big role in opening his eyes at an early age to the challenges and rewards of the restaurant business. While he was in high school, Edward worked at the Terrace Five in Trump Tower and later helped his family operate and sell a midtown Manhattan restaurant. Edward continued his culinary training under famed New York chef Frank Crispo. He took over a failing Chinese restaurant in 1998 and turned it into his own place, Clay; he transformed it into a stylish, Asian-inspired restaurant. Clay attracted national and international media attention and put Lee on the map at the age of twenty-five. Five years later, he sold Clay and made Kentucky his home.

Having grown up in a Korean neighborhood in Brooklyn, I learned the importance of tradition, family, and community early on in my life. As a teenager, when most of my friends were playing soccer and football, I preferred standing alongside my grandmother watching and helping her prepare dinner. Little did I know she was teaching me the basic principles of Korean cooking, such as pickling vegetables, curing and drying fish, and marinating meats. And my Korean roots still find their way onto my menu in subtle ways, such as homemade pickles and cured meats. I still feel my grandmother's dedication and love of cooking guiding me to this day in my culinary pursuits and aspirations.

Photographer
martin**vandiver**

Food Stylist
kris**ackerman**

...every meal is a narrative

halibut **en papillote**

recipesrecipes

Halibut en Papillote

Bibb Lettuce Salad with Fresh Peaches, Spiced Pecans and

Blue Cheese Dressing

Watermelon Lavender Soup with Yogurt Sorbet

Bourbon Cherries with Ricotta Cheese and Marjoram

edward**lee** 89

halibut en papillote

serves **4**

4 (6-ounce) portions halibut
8 pearl onions
16 asparagus tips
16 teardrop tomatoes
16 wax beans
4 teaspoons chopped thyme
4 teaspoons lemon juice
1/4 cup (1/2 stick) butter
1/2 cup (4 ounces) dry vermouth
salt and pepper to taste
1 cup water

Place 4 pieces of parchment paper flat on a work table. Place 1 portion of halibut in the middle of each parchment sheet. Arrange 2 pearl onions, 4 asparagus tips, 4 teardrop tomatoes, and 4 wax beans on top of each portion. Sprinkle each with 1 teaspoon thyme and drizzle with 1 teaspoon lemon juice. Top with 1 tablespoon butter and drizzle with 2 tablespoons dry vermouth. Sprinkle with salt and pepper.

Bring together the top and bottom edges of the parchment paper and fold over about 1/2 inch; push down on the paper so that it gently presses flat against the fish. Twist the right and left sides of the parchment paper as you would a candy wrapper. Bring the right and left ends together so that they fold over the top of the parchment package.

Preheat the oven to 400 degrees. Pour the water into a 10-inch ovenproof sauté pan. Place the parchment packages gently in the water bath. Place the pan in the oven and bake for 25 to 30 minutes.

Take the sauté pan out of the oven and use oven mitts to grab each parchment package and place on 4 warmed plates. Rip open the middle of the package just before serving, taking care to keep your face away from the top of the parchment package because hot steam will escape from the package when ripped open. Serve the fish in the parchment on the plate.

Being a chef today, I feel a great personal responsibility to not only provide a gracious dining experience but also to educate my guests. I believe that a meal should restore health, vigor, excitement, and perhaps a good memory to people on their journey through life.

That is why I have taken an active role in farming and have commissioned one of my staff members, Mindy Weisman, a fourth-generation farmer, to help me launch Magnolia Farms. A six-acre farm in Indiana, Magnolia Farms produces vegetables and herbs for the restaurant, but we have taken the farm a step further by researching and reintroducing once-forgotten edible herbs, plants, and flowers.

My personal mission is to reintroduce these ingredients, discover delicious ways to highlight their unique qualities, and make diners more aware of these eclectic plants. Whether guests simply discover a new taste sensation or decide to pick up gardening as a way of enjoying the outdoors, I will feel that I have given back in my own special way—sharing a piece of tradition and myself with those sitting in my dining room.

bibb lettuce salad with fresh peaches, spiced pecans and blue cheese dressing

serves **4**

4 heads Bibb lettuce
4 ripe peaches
blue cheese dressing
spiced pecans

Cut out the core of each head of Bibb lettuce with a small paring knife so that the leaves will easily pull apart. Skin each peach and slice into thin wedges.

Place 1 head of Bibb lettuce on each of 4 chilled plates. Arrange the wedges of peaches in between the lettuce leaves. Drizzle about ¼ cup blue cheese dressing on each head of lettuce and sprinkle with a handful of spiced pecans. Serve immediately.

blue cheese dressing

12 ounces blue cheese
2 teaspoons heavy cream
½ quart mayonnaise
2 tablespoons Dijon mustard
1 tablespoon crème fraîche
1 teaspoon lemon juice
1 teaspoon sherry vinegar
pinch of white pepper
pinch of salt

Combine the blue cheese and heavy cream in a 12-inch sauté pan and gently heat over a low flame, stirring with a wooden spoon until the cheese melts and combines with the heavy cream. Take off the heat and let cool for about 10 minutes. Transfer to a bowl and gently fold in the mayonnaise, mustard, crème fraîche, lemon juice and sherry vinegar.

Add a pinch each of salt and pepper. Let chill in the refrigerator for 30 minutes.

spiced pecans

6 tablespoons (¾ cup) butter
1 pound pecans
¼ cup sugar
1 tablespoon spice mix of equal parts cinnamon, cumin, paprika, ground caraway, white pepper and nutmeg

Heat the butter in a large sauté pan until foamy. Add the pecans and sugar and toss to coat. Add the spice mix and shake the pan until all the pecans are thoroughly coated with the spice mix. Cook for about 10 minutes or until the butter has been absorbed and the pecans are roasted, continuing to shake the pan. Drain on a paper towel and let cool. This will make more than you need for the recipe; store the remaining pecans in an airtight container.

watermelon lavender soup
with yogurt sorbet

serves **4**

1 small watermelon
1 cup sugar
1 1/4 cups water
1/2 cup dried lavender
yogurt sorbet
4 teaspoons ground pistachio nuts, for garnish

Slice the watermelon into halves. Spoon out the flesh and put into a blender. Pulse until the watermelon turns to liquid, being careful not to blend too much or the juice will become too foamy. Measure 2 quarts watermelon juice.

Combine the sugar and water in a saucepan and bring to a boil for exactly 2 minutes. Remove from the heat and let cool for about 10 minutes. Add the dried lavender to the sugar water and let steep for half an hour. Strain and combine the lavender syrup with the watermelon juice in a large container. Chill in the refrigerator for 1 hour to overnight.

Divide the watermelon soup evenly among 4 chilled bowls. Add a scoop of yogurt sorbet to each bowl. Sprinkle with the ground pistachio nuts and serve immediately.

yogurt sorbet
1/4 cup sugar
1/4 cup fresh apple juice
1 teaspoon honey
1 cup (8 ounces) yogurt

Combine the sugar, apple juice and honey in a medium saucepan and bring to a boil for exactly 2 minutes. Remove from the heat and let cool for 15 minutes. Transfer to a bowl and gently fold in the yogurt. Chill the mixture for 1 hour to overnight. Freeze the mixture in an ice cream maker, using the manufacturer's instructions.

For this soup you can substitute your favorite frozen yogurt or even just a scoop of chilled sweetened yogurt if you don't have an ice cream maker.

bourbon cherries
with ricotta cheese and marjoram

serves **4**

8 ounces fresh ricotta cheese
2 tablespoons confectioners' sugar
1 teaspoon grated lemon zest
1 teaspoon vanilla extract
2 teaspoons chopped fresh marjoram
3 tablespoons butter
12 ounces pitted cherries
2 tablespoons light brown sugar
1/2 cup bourbon, aged at least 8 years

Combine the ricotta cheese, confectioners' sugar, lemon zest and vanilla in a mixer bowl and cream together. Fold in the chopped marjoram gently. Chill in the refrigerator for 1 hour.

Heat the butter in a 12-inch sauté pan until foamy. Add the cherries and brown sugar and toss until the cherries are coated. Remove from the heat and, making sure to protect your face, gently add the bourbon to the saucepan.

Return the pan to the heat and stay clear of the pan because the bourbon will ignite and flame. Cook for about 4 minutes until the flames go out and the bourbon reduces to a syrup.

Divide the ricotta mixture evenly among 4 chilled plates. Spoon the cherries evenly over the ricotta, drizzling the remaining syrup over the cherries. Serve immediately.

Food has always been synonymous with celebrations for me, so much so that I made a deal with my parents that they would take me to a fancy dinner each year to celebrate my birthday. I dined at some of the most acclaimed restaurants in Manhattan, and I can still vividly recall memories of The Sign of the Dove, China Grille, Gotham Bar & Grill, and many more.

At that time, it never dawned on me that the world my grandmother and I shared in our windowless kitchen in Brooklyn and the world of those fancy chefs behind those sacred closed doors were not all that far apart. After all, cooking is rooted in shared tradition and technique. After many years of cooking, reading, traveling, and stretching my imagination, I finally understood that cooking is a limitless process and a privilege. And whether a dish is served on French porcelain china or in a familiar chipped ceramic bowl, delicious food is about sharing a piece of yourself with others.

benjamin**mccallum**

Chef Benjamin McCallum is a principal owner and executive chef of Three Sons Kitchen, a full-service, by-design catering firm in Minneapolis, Minnesota.

This small, family-owned and -operated catering team specializes in creating unique menus for each client, reflecting the client's culture, personality, and budget.

McCallum was born on April 27, 1976, in Minneapolis, Minnesota. He moved with his parents and two brothers to a goat farm in Kentucky two years later. Mom and Dad built the farm with their own hands, while the brothers worked at chores from sunup to sundown.

Benjamin's mom taught him the art of making cheese and other dairy products, and his father, a professional chef himself, taught him every other aspect of culinary preparation and presentation. The three brothers moved back to Minneapolis in 1988, where Benjamin's training under his father became more intensive.

Benjamin was head chef at Café Camarda in Mankato, Minnesota, and associate chef for Dayton's Design Cuisine in Minneapolis, now known as Marshall Field's Design Cuisine, before starting his own catering company with his brothers in 2000.

I always possessed a great love for food.

Watching my father prepare dinners at home awed me when I was young. I was transfixed by the complexity of creating the perfect stock and pairing ideal ingredients.

What I like best about preparing an incredible meal is the instant gratification I get from happy guests. From the moment the palate detects genuinely good food, the rest of the body displays emotions. As a result, the chef is in a unique position to "test-market" new creations with friends and family who do not feel the need to hold back on their own reactions to food. I think food brings us closer together. My wife and I can have an argument, but she always forgets why as soon as she tastes one of my sauces.

Photographer
dianepadys

Food Stylist
christynordstrom

macadamia-crusted halibut

recipesrecipes

Macadamia-Crusted Halibut with Roasted Red Pepper Beurre Blanc Sauce

Field Greens with Apples, Strawberries, Herbed Chèvre and Candied Pecans

in a Champagne Vinaigrette

benjaminmccallum 95

macadamia-crusted halibut
with roasted red pepper beurre blanc sauce

serves **6**

2 cups macadamias
1 cup bread crumbs
2 teaspoons salt
2 teaspoons pepper
1 1/2 cups all-purpose flour
6 (6- to 8-ounce) halibut steaks
2 cups buttermilk
3 cups soybean oil
roasted red pepper beurre blanc sauce

roasted red pepper beurre blanc sauce
8 ounces whole sweet red peppers
1 tablespoon olive oil
2 ounces chopped shallots
2 ounces chopped garlic
3 cups Pinot Grigio
1 cup fish stock
1/2 cup (1 stick) butter, softened

Pulse the macadamias in a food processor or blender until coarsely chopped. Add the bread crumbs slowly, processing until the mixture becomes coarse crumbs; if the nuts become clumpy, add more bread crumbs. Remove to a small bowl and set aside.

Preheat the oven to 350 degrees. Mix the salt, pepper and flour in a small bowl.

Soak the halibut in the buttermilk in a bowl for 5 minutes. Remove the steaks and press one side into the flour mixture. Return the fish to the buttermilk flour side down and quickly remove again. Press the same side down into the macadamia mixture. Set aside and repeat for each steak.

Bring the soybean oil to medium-high heat in a deep sauté pan. Place the crusted sides of the halibut steaks in the hot oil and cook until the crust browns, 2 to 3 minutes. Remove the steaks from the oil with tongs, taking care not to damage the crust, and place on a sheet pan crust side up.

Roast in the preheated oven for 10 to 15 minutes, or until cooked throughout.

Pour the sauce onto each plate and place 1 halibut steak crust side up in the center of the sauce.

Roast the whole red peppers over an open flame or on a grill until the skin blackens. Plunge into cold water to stop the cooking process, then remove the charred skin, stem and seeds. Heat the olive oil in a sauté pan. Add the chopped shallots and garlic and sauté until light brown. Deglaze the sauté pan with some of the wine and then add the remaining wine and fish stock. Add the peppers to the sauté pan and simmer for 10 to 15 minutes.

Pour the mixture into a blender and blend until smooth. Return the sauce to the sauté pan and place over low heat. Add the butter to the sauce gradually, whisking until thoroughly combined.

field greens
with apples, strawberries, herbed chèvre and candied pecans in a champagne vinaigrette

serves **6**

15 ounces spring field greens mix
champagne vinaigrette
1 Granny Smith apple
6 medium-large strawberries
6 ounces herbed chèvre
candied pecans

Clean the field greens and toss with the vinaigrette in a bowl. Spoon onto serving plates. Cut the apple and strawberries into 1/8-inch slices and place over the field greens.

Cut a corner off the chèvre package and squeeze the strings of cheese onto the salad. Placing the soft cheese in a pastry or sandwich bag and cutting one corner would work as well. Sprinkle the candied pecans over the top and serve.

champagne vinaigrette
2 tablespoons Champagne vinegar
1/2 teaspoon mustard
1/2 teaspoon honey
6 tablespoons olive oil

Mix the vinegar, mustard and honey in a small bowl. Add the olive oil slowly in a steady stream, whisking constantly with a balloon whisk until thoroughly mixed.

candied pecans
1/2 cup chopped pecans
1/2 cup sugar

Place the chopped pecans in a small pile on a cookie sheet. Melt the sugar in a saucepan, stirring often and cooking just until the sugar liquefies and turns amber or light brown.

Pour the liquid sugar over the pecans immediately and let stand for 15 to 20 minutes until cool. Place a piece of waxed or parchment paper over the candied pecans and crush with a meat tenderizer or other weighted object until the pecans are very fine.

sven-erik**mill**

Mill was born in Sweden and started his professional career in 1972 in the kitchen of Loka Brunn (a resort that got its royal privilege from King Adolf Fredrik in 1632) under the leadership of Gert Klötzke, a chef and the force behind the Swedish National Culinary Team.

Sven-Erik became master of barbecue at the resort. Mill was in charge of everything prepared and served outside the Loka Brunn kitchen, becoming familiar with young and talented chefs from all over Sweden. Today, the mines for which the area was famous are closed, and steel production is mostly automated. The area has gone from mining to dining, from steel to meal, and Sven-Erik's company, Mill's Ost & Vilt (Mill's Cheese & Game), has became one of the major brands contributing to the new era, using the fresh produce of the region.

The company's Grythytte Blue is an organic blue cow's milk cheese now stocked by every gourmet food market in Stockholm. He produces air-dried wild boar that challenges the best Parma hams, Pata Nergas, cloudberry wine-marinated steaks from elk or venison, and sausage. Many of the products are used by the Michelin two-starred restaurant Edsbacka and other fine restaurants, including the Grand Hotel's French restaurant in the heart of Stockholm, Fond in Gothenburg, the Grythyttan Gästgivaregård, and many others. For five years, His Royal Highness the King of Sweden has used Sven-Erik's services, and for the last three years, Sven-Erik has delivered a buffet to the King's celebration of the Swedish National Day.

...*learned to value quality and freshness*

Riding my bicycle to my mother's job in the kitchen of Sikfors manor, I passed through dark, blue-green woodlands, caught the scent of flowers in the fields, and was hypnotized by the silvery sparkles from the lakes. All the guesthouses and manors in this mining area were founded with iron and steel fortunes. And my mother was one of the best-known cooks, using game, mushrooms, and berries from the woods and fields, and fish and crawfish from the many fresh lakes. I followed her profession closely and, in the process, learned to value quality and freshness.

Photographer: **jimmcfarlane**

Food Stylist: **janetlillie**

grythytte **stew**

recipesrecipes

Grythytte Stew

Sweet Rosemary Apples

sven-erik**mill** 99

grythytte stew

I run a small business producing cheese and wild game charcuterie and serving guests in my tavern in the heart of the Swedish woodlands between sparkling lakes.

serves 6

3¹/₃ pounds venison
5 tablespoons corn oil or canola oil
2 tablespoons butter
1¹/₄ cups red table wine
2 large Spanish onions
3 large ribs celery
3 fresh ripe tomatoes or canned tomatoes
2 tablespoons corn oil or canola oil
2 tablespoons butter
2¹/₂ liters dark broth, game stock or beef stock
12 whole white peppercorns
10 juniper berries, slightly crushed
2 stems fresh thyme
2 bay leaves
tawny port sauce with cherries
3 tablespoons brown sugar

Chop the venison into 1-inch pieces. Fry until brown in 5 tablespoons corn oil and 2 tablespoons butter in a large sauté pan. Remove from the pan. Pour in the wine and reduce for approximately 5 minutes until almost dry.

Chop the onions, celery and tomatoes into quarters. Add to the sauté pan with 2 tablespoons corn oil and 2 tablespoons butter. Sauté until the vegetables are light brown. Return the venison to the sauté pan. Add the broth, white peppercorns, juniper berries, thyme and bay leaves. Simmer for 40 minutes. Take out the venison meat.

Cook the sauce until reduced to the desired thickness and your desired intensity in taste. Strain the sauce and combine with the venison in the sauté pan; keep warm.

Stir the desired amount of the tawny port sauce into the stew to flavor it. Return the cherries to the saucepan with the small amount of tawny port sauce remaining in the saucepan and add the brown sugar. Sauté until the brown sugar dissolves and forms a syrup.

Serve the cherries over the stew. Serve with boiled new potatoes and accompany with beer or a heavy-bodied red wine.

tawny port sauce with cherries
peel of 1 orange, bitter white pith removed
peel of 1 lemon, bitter white pith removed
1¹/₄ cups tawny port
1¹/₄ cups red table wine
5 ounces black currant liqueur
2 tablespoons black currant jelly
1.8 pounds pitted cherries

Chop the orange peel and lemon peel and place in a small sachet; tie the bag shut. Combine with the port, red wine, liqueur and jelly in a saucepan. Bring to a boil. Add the cherries and simmer for 5 minutes. Remove the cherries with a slotted spoon to use as a garnish for the stew. Cook the liquid to reduce and remove from the heat.

sweet **rosemary apples**

serves **6**

6 apples
5 tablespoons butter
2 (6-inch) sprigs fresh rosemary
3 tablespoons brown sugar
maple lemon sauce
6 (3¹/₂-ounce) portions blue cheese, deep-fried
    in corn oil or canola oil (optional)

Cut each apple into 8 wedges. Fry the wedges
in the butter in a sauté pan until brown. Add
the rosemary and sprinkle with the brown
sugar. Sauté until the apples are candied.
Remove the rosemary and serve immediately
or at room temperature with the maple lemon
sauce. Top each serving with fried blue cheese
if desired.

maple lemon sauce

grated zest and juice of 1 lemon
10 tablespoons crème fraîche
¹/₄ cup maple syrup

Combine the lemon zest, lemon juice, crème
fraîche and syrup in a bowl and stir to mix
well. Cover and chill in the refrigerator.

walter**potenza**

Walter Potenza was born in Giulianova, Abruzzo, Italy, and attended Villa Santa Maria Culinary School in Chieti, Italy. He emigrated to the United States and worked in some of New England's finest restaurants before opening his own, Walter's in East Greenwich, in 1987.

Potenza currently operates several restaurants in Providence, Rhode Island, a cooking school in Providence, and Etruria International Cooking School in Gubbio, Italy. He is an avid researcher of the history of ancient gastronomy and enology and, in 2002, opened Walter's Historical Fine Dining, a restaurant featuring authentic cuisine from different periods of Italian history, from the Roman Empire to the unification of Italy in 1865. His most recent cookbook, *Federal Hill Flavors and Knowledge,* and the soon-to-be released *Nineteen Ghettos: The Food of the Jews in Italy* are in-depth explorations of historical cuisines. As part of his research, he has discovered and introduced Americans to terra-cotta cookery, an ancient cooking method invented by the Etruscans 300 years before the Roman Empire.

He has appeared in national and international publications, as well as on television and radio. His articles are featured in Italian gastronomic magazines and on the Internet. He hosts a cooking show, *Stir It Up,* on Cox Cable and has appeared on the Food Network. He is currently working on a new historical television show and the nationwide launch of his new line of terra-cotta cookware.

We cook who we are; imagine being able to make humankind smile by simply understanding their religion, traditions, memories, and land of origin and transferring those emotions into great cuisine.

Photographer &
Food Stylist
arlene**tavoroff**

We cook who we are.

crepe molds

recipesrecipes

Crepe Molds Filled with Shrimp, Mushrooms and Tarragon

   Béchamel Sauce

White Swiss Chard Tart

Fresh Artichokes Filled with Lamb and Duck Confit

Gratin of Zucchini, Fennel and Amaretti

crepe molds filled with shrimp, mushrooms and tarragon béchamel sauce

serves 6

2 ribs celery, sliced
2 leeks, white parts only, sliced
2 carrots, sliced
1 cup sliced oyster mushrooms or shiitake
    mushrooms
salt and black pepper to taste
1 tablespoon fresh tarragon
2 tablespoons unsalted butter
18 shrimp, peeled and deveined
1/3 cup dry white wine
béchamel sauce
18 crepes
3 tablespoons grated Parmigiano-
    Reggiano cheese
2 tablespoons unsalted butter

Sauté the celery, leeks, carrots, mushrooms, salt, pepper and tarragon in 2 tablespoons butter in a saucepan. Add the shrimp and wine and cook until the wine evaporates. Fold in the béchamel sauce.

Preheat the oven to 500 degrees. Butter 6 individual soufflé dishes or ramekins. Line each with 3 crepes, layer with the shrimp, and top with the cheese and 2 tablespoons butter. Bake until hot and light brown. Invert onto serving plates and serve hot with a sauce of saffron, a touch of mascarpone and prosecco wine.

béchamel sauce
2 tablespoons unsalted butter
3 tablespoons all-purpose flour
1 cup whole milk

Melt the butter in a saucepan. Add the flour and cook over medium heat for 4 minutes, stirring constantly. Whisk in the milk and cook until boiling and thick, whisking constantly.

crepes
2 whole eggs
1 cup unbleached all-purpose flour
salt to taste
1 cup whole milk
1 1/4 tablespoons unsalted butter, melted,
    plus extra for cooking the crepes

Combine the eggs, flour and salt in a bowl. Add the milk, whisking constantly. Whisk in the butter. Heat a lightly buttered pan and pour in a little batter, tilting the pan to spread out the batter. Cook until golden brown on both sides, about 1 minute, turning once. Repeat with the remaining batter. You should have 18 crepes. You can prepare the crepes up to 3 days in advance.

white **swiss chard** tart

Of Ligurian origin, specifically from the city of Genova, this tart can also be made with onions. It was a favorite dish for Sabbath, made ahead of time and kept on the counter overnight. Catholics in Liguria make something similar for Easter with quail eggs and spinach, called Torta Pasqualina.

serves 8

1 medium zucchini, washed and chopped
1 bunch white Swiss chard, leaves only,
    washed and sliced
1 rib celery, chopped
3 scallions, sliced
2 large eggs
kosher salt and freshly ground black pepper
    to taste
$1/2$ cup (2 ounces) freshly grated Parmigiano-
    Reggiano cheese
$1/4$ cup extra-virgin olive oil
tart pastry
8 small eggs
1 tablespoon extra-virgin olive oil

Preheat the oven to 350 degrees. Mix the zucchini, Swiss chard, celery, scallions, 2 eggs, salt, pepper, cheese and $1/4$ cup olive oil. Spoon into the pastry-lined pan and make 8 little wells for the small eggs. Break the eggs into the wells and season with salt and pepper.

Top with the second disk of dough and roll the excess dough to form a little rope around the edge of the tart. Brush the top with 1 tablespoon olive oil; pierce a few times with a fork to prevent a bubble from forming. Bake for 30 minutes, or until the top crust begins to turn golden brown. Serve warm or at room temperature.

tart pastry
$1 1/2$ cups unbleached all-purpose flour
$1/8$ teaspoon kosher salt
$1/3$ cup plus 1 tablespoon cool water
$1/4$ cup extra-virgin olive oil

Pile the flour on a counter, making a well in the center. Add the salt, cool water and 3 tablespoons of the olive oil to the well and mix with a fork until the ingredients begin to come together.

Knead the dough until it is smooth and elastic, about 5 minutes, adding a little water if it is dry or a little flour if it is sticky; wrap and let it rest for 20 minutes.

Roll the dough out into 2 thin disks, one slightly larger than the other, on a lightly floured counter. Brush a 12-inch tart pan with the remaining 1 tablespoon olive oil and line the pan with the larger disk of dough, being careful not to rip the dough.

fresh artichokes
filled with lamb and duck confit

serves **4**

1 large onion, minced
2 tablespoons extra-virgin olive oil
4 ounces boneless skinless duck breast, chopped
4 ounces lamb shoulder, chopped
1/4 cup dry white wine
3 cups vegetable broth
2 slices Italian bread
1 cup whole milk
1 tablespoon minced Italian parsley
salt and black pepper to taste
4 medium artichokes, trimmed
1 shallot, minced
2 tomatoes, peeled, seeded and chopped
2 tablespoons extra-virgin olive oil

Sauté the onion in 2 tablespoons olive oil in a sauté pan over medium heat until it is translucent, about 5 minutes. Add the duck and lamb and cook, stirring, until lightly browned, about 5 minutes.

Deglaze the sauté pan with the wine and cook until the wine evaporates. Add 1 cup of the broth and simmer until all the liquid has been absorbed, about 15 minutes.

Soak the bread in the milk in a bowl and squeeze dry; crumble into the bowl of a food processor and add the duck and lamb with any cooking juice left in the pan. Add the parsley, salt and pepper and process to a paste; cool to room temperature.

Remove the hairy choke from each artichoke. Stuff each artichoke with the meat mixture and place in a deep pan; add the shallot and tomatoes. Drizzle with 2 tablespoons olive oil and add enough of the remaining broth to come halfway up the artichokes; season with salt and pepper and cover. Cook over medium heat for 40 minutes or until done to taste, checking for tenderness by pulling the outer leaves.

Serve the artichokes with their own broth and finish with hot pepper olive oil and a julienne of fresh red beets.

gratin of zucchini, fennel and amaretti

serves **4**

2 tablespoons olive oil

2 tablespoons plain bread crumbs

2 medium zucchini, sliced into $^1/_4$-inch rounds

$^1/_2$ teaspoon freshly ground black pepper

1 teaspoon kosher salt

1 tablespoon finely chopped flat-leaf
  Italian parsley

2 medium fennel bulbs

$^1/_2$ cup whole milk

3 tablespoons all-purpose flour, sifted

$^1/_8$ teaspoon freshly grated or ground nutmeg

$^1/_2$ cup (2 ounces) shredded Gruyère cheese

$^1/_2$ cup (2 ounces) grated Parmigiano-
  Reggiano cheese

$2^1/_2$ teaspoons kosher salt

$^1/_2$ teaspoon freshly ground black pepper

$^1/_3$ cup ground amaretti

Soak a Timballo terra-cotta pot in cold water for 15 minutes; drain. Pour 1 tablespoon of the olive oil into the center of the Timballo pot and use your fingers to rub the oil around the center and side of the pot. Add the bread crumbs and shake the pot to dust evenly.

Drizzle the zucchini slices with the remaining 1 tablespoon olive oil in a bowl. Add $^1/_2$ teaspoon pepper, 1 teaspoon salt and the parsley; toss lightly. Layer evenly in the Timballo pot. Cut the fennel into halves lengthwise. Remove the center cores and cut the fennel into $^1/_8$-inch slices. Layer over the zucchini.

Preheat the oven to 350 degrees. Combine the milk, flour, nutmeg, Gruyère cheese, Parmigiano-Reggiano cheese, $2^1/_2$ teaspoons salt and $^1/_2$ teaspoon pepper in a mixing bowl and whisk together. Pour the mixture over the vegetables and let stand for 5 minutes. Top with the ground amaretti. Bake for 45 minutes or until set and creamy.

norapouillon

Nora Pouillon merges gourmet cuisine with her passion for sustainable agriculture and vibrant health in her work, which is a reflection of her philosophy, "Spend on food what you save on the doctor."

Nora was born in Vienna, and her commitment to healthy eating began with her parents, who believed in serving their family simply prepared meals made with top-quality seasonal ingredients. She has traveled widely and brings the inspiration of these journeys to her table. She has utilized this background as the internationally acclaimed owner of two successful restaurants in Washington, D.C., Nora and Asia Nora, serving multi-ethnic, organically produced food. Nora was the first certified organic restaurant in the country and has been heralded in publications from coast to coast, including the *Mobil Travel Guide*, which awarded it four stars in 2001, and the *Zagat Survey*, in which it is consistently rated one of the top ten restaurants. Nora Pouillon was voted Chef of the Year by the IACP in 1997.

She is active in many organizations, such as Chefs Collaborative, which supports environmentally sustainable living, and the Natural Resources Defense Council's "Give North Atlantic Swordfish a Break" campaign. *Cooking with Nora*, her cookbook, was a finalist for the IACP/Julia Child Cookbook Awards.

The inspiration to serve simple, organic cuisine is rooted in my childhood, when I lived on a farm my father rented in the mountains in Tyrol, in western Austria. The farmer and his family that lived with us had a completely self-sufficient lifestyle, working from morning until evening just to feed themselves. I began to realize how precious food was; it provided the basis for optimum health, which farm life requires.

Are our modern lives so different that our food doesn't matter anymore? I don't think so. Juggling long work hours, family, traffic, pollution, etc.—these contemporary stresses require the same healthful, natural food that our parents and grandparents ate while working the land. And I'm convinced that organic food not only tastes better but is also qualitatively superior in every way, including nutritional content.

Photographer
sean**fitzgerald**

Food Stylist
lisa**goldenschroeder**

sake-glazed **wild salmon**

Spend on food what you save on the doctor:

recipesrecipes

Sake-Glazed Wild Salmon with Miso Yuzu Vinaigrette

Belgian Endive, Mâche, Beet and Apple Salad with Walnuts and
  Sherry Vinaigrette

sake-glazed wild salmon
with miso yuzu vinaigrette

Yuzu is a sour Japanese citrus fruit used to enhance flavor. It can be found in Japanese groceries.

serves **4**

1/4 cup sake
1/4 cup mirin
2 tablespoons (or less) sugar
1/2 cup white miso
4 (4- to 5-ounce) wild salmon fillets
1 tablespoon sunflower oil or safflower oil
stir-fried vegetables
miso yuzu vinaigrette
crisp-fried fresh spaghettini strands

Combine the sake, mirin and sugar in a saucepan and cook until the alcohol evaporates and the sugar dissolves, about 2 to 3 minutes. Whisk in the miso and cool.

Arrange the salmon in a single layer in a flat-bottomed plastic or stainless steel pan. Cover with a moistened cheesecloth and pour the sake mixture over the top, spreading to cover evenly. Marinate in the refrigerator for 3 hours to overnight.

Heat the sunflower oil in a sauté pan. Lift the cheesecloth and residual marinade from the fish and discard. Place the fish glazed side down in the pan and sear until caramelized.

Turn the fish carefully and cook for 3 to 4 minutes longer or until done, or finish in a preheated 450-degree oven.

Serve over tatsoi, bok choy, carrots or red peppers stir-fried with garlic and ginger in sunflower oil or spinach stir-fried with garlic, ginger and sesame seeds. Drizzle the miso yuzu vinaigrette around the vegetables and top with crisply fried fresh spaghettini.

miso yuzu vinaigrette
1/4 cup white miso
3 tablespoons yuzu juice or lemon juice
1 tablespoon tamari or soy sauce
2 tablespoons chopped fresh ginger,
    about 1 (2-inch) piece
1/4 cup water
1 teaspoon ground black pepper
6 to 8 tablespoons sunflower oil or safflower oil

Process the miso, yuzu juice, tamari, ginger, water and pepper in a blender until smooth. Add the sunflower oil gradually, processing constantly to emulsify.

Over the years, first as a home cook, later as a caterer, and then as a chef and restaurateur, I have been asked how I prepare my food and why it tastes so good. The key to success with any recipe is to find the freshest organic ingredients and prepare them simply, allowing the cook more time to share with family and friends. To me, this is as important as the meal itself, because while food nourishes our bodies, leisurely dining with good company truly nourishes the soul.

belgian endive, mâche, beet and apple salad
with walnuts and sherry vinaigrette

serves **4**

8 small beets, about 8 ounces
¼ cup English walnut halves
4 to 6 ounces mâche or watercress,
    washed and spun dry
sherry vinaigrette
4 heads Belgian endive
1 apple, thinly sliced

Steam the beets for 12 to 15 minutes in a small covered saucepan with a collapsible steamer; allow to cool. Peel and cut into quarters.

Preheat the oven to 350 degrees. Spread the walnuts on a baking sheet and bake for 8 to 10 minutes or until fragrant and toasted.

Toss the mâche with some of the sherry vinaigrette. Divide the greens among 4 dinner-size plates, placing them in the centers of the plates. Wipe the Belgian endive with a damp cloth, trim the base, and separate the leaves. Arrange the endive leaves and apple slices around the greens. Add the beets to each salad and sprinkle with the walnuts. Drizzle the remaining sherry vinaigrette over the endive leaves.

sherry vinaigrette
1 tablespoon sherry vinegar
sea salt and freshly ground black pepper
    to taste
3 tablespoons extra-virgin olive oil

Combine the sherry vinegar with salt and pepper in a small bowl and stir until the salt dissolves. Add the olive oil slowly, whisking constantly with a fork.

christopher**prosperi**

Christopher Prosperi is the chef and owner of the award-winning Metro Bis restaurant in Simsbury, Connecticut, where he specializes in American bistro cuisine, combining flavors, herbs, and spices from around the world while maintaining the integrity of their original cuisines.

Items such as spring rolls, smoked salmon, goat cheese tarts, Maryland lump crab "cocktail," and foie gras are comfortably situated on the Metro Bis menu with traditional favorites. The diversity of the menu is reflective of his culinary career and upbringing. His French father is a pastry chef who teaches at the Culinary Institute of America, and his Austrian mother was a restaurant manager. He has referenced this foundation since graduating from the CIA and working at the West Street Grill in Litchfield, Connecticut, and Mark's Place in Miami.

Chef Prosperi is a frequent guest on a variety of televised cooking segments and teaches regular classes on American bistro cuisine at the Mystic Cooking School and The Silo in New Milford, Connecticut. He co-authors a weekly column in the *Hartford Courant* on the basics of cooking with Bill Daley, food writer for the *Chicago Tribune* and president of the Association of Food Journalists. A book comprised of these columns is currently in the proposal stage. Prosperi's recipes are also included in a number of books, including *Wife of the Chef: The True Story of a Restaurant and Romance* by his wife, Courtney Febbroriello.

Chef Prosperi has prepared a dinner at the James Beard House three times and also bottles his original salad dressings under the Prosperi label. Prosperi's first love is the kitchen, where he integrates his culinary experiences to create the menu at Metro Bis, and "the holy joy of creation literally lights up his face as he works the stove."

My wife, Courtney Febbroriello, captures my love of food better than I ever could in her book, Wife of the Chef: The True Story of a Restaurant and Romance. *Courtney wrote this ten years ago, when we first met. When she read it to me later, I was shocked by how she could almost see inside me.*

"Rhythmic grace. Fluidity of movement. Intense concentration. Respect of materials. Paying attention to everything that goes on but seems to be involved in his own world. Touching and tasting everything. Looking at a consommé curiously to see how it will come out. The wonder of food. A complete grasp and the knowledge of what to expect. The joy of discovering or creating something new."

Photographer
traceymaurer

Food Stylist
maryellen**rose**

My passion for food is like listening to my heart beat.

oven-roasted **rainbow trout**

recipesrecipes

Oven-Roasted Rainbow Trout with Spring Vegetable Ragout and Spring Pea Sauce

Spring Vegetable and Crab Soup

Crab Cocktail

Pear Panna Cotta with Pear William Eau de Vie

christopher**prosperi** 113

oven-roasted rainbow trout
with spring vegetable ragout and spring pea sauce

serves 6

Each spring, I am asked for recipes that highlight the seasonal, local ingredients of Connecticut. I love the bite of fiddlehead ferns and the earthy richness of morel mushrooms, but the rainbow trout is my favorite, and it reminds me of those careless spring days spent fishing with my brothers. When I tested this recipe, I was amazed at how well all of the flavors came together, and it quickly found a place on our spring menu.

6 (4-ounce) trout fillets
salt to taste
1 tablespoon good quality extra-virgin olive oil

1/2 lemon
spring vegetable ragout
spring pea sauce (page 117)

Preheat the oven to 375 degrees. Line a baking sheet with foil. Season the fish with a sprinkle of salt on both sides and place skin side up on the pan. Drizzle with the olive oil and squeeze the juice from the lemon on the fillets. Bake in the oven for 5 to 7 minutes or until cooked through.

Place the spring vegetable ragout on a warm serving platter and top with the fish fillets. Serve the spring pea sauce on the side. You may also evenly divide on individual plates and encircle the vegetables with the sauce.

spring vegetable ragout

1 pound asparagus, about 1 bunch
1 gallon water
1/2 cup kosher salt
1 cup shelled fava beans
1 cup shelled spring peas
1/2 cup fiddlehead ferns (optional)
1 tablespoon extra-virgin olive oil
1 1/2 to 2 cups (1/2-inch pieces) Vidalia onion, about 1 (6- to 8-ounce) onion

1/2 teaspoon kosher salt
1 pound fresh morels, cut into halves and rinsed well
1 cup cream sherry
1/2 cup low-sodium chicken stock
1 tablespoon cornstarch
1 tablespoon cold water
1 tablespoon butter
kosher salt and black pepper to taste

Bend the asparagus toward the end of the stalk and it will break at the natural spot where it is freshest. Discard the lower part or save for making soup. Line up the spears and cut into 1-inch pieces.

Bring 1 gallon water to a rolling boil in an 8-quart pot and add 1/2 cup salt. Place the asparagus in the water and blanch for 1 minute. Fish out all the asparagus with a strainer and set aside on a plate. Allow the water to return to a vigorous boil and repeat three more times with the fava beans, spring peas and optional fiddlehead ferns, placing one type of vegetable in the water at a time.

Heat the olive oil in a 4-quart pot over medium heat and stir in the Vidalia onion. Season with 1/2 teaspoon salt and sauté for 2 to 3 minutes. Add the morel halves and cook for an additional 1 to 2 minutes. Deglaze with the cream sherry and reduce until almost dry. Pour in the chicken stock and bring to a simmer.

Blend the cornstarch with 1 tablespoon cold water in a cup to create a slurry and pour into the simmering stock and vegetables while stirring. Cook until thickened, stirring constantly. Add the rest of the vegetables and finish with the butter. Adjust the seasoning with salt and a few grinds of black pepper.

spring vegetable and crab soup

I love soups because they are so easy to make, and they easily showcase the flavors of the current season. This spring vegetable soup can be made ahead of time and reheated later; I think it tastes best when the ingredients have had a chance to meld. The vegetables can also be prepared the day before and stored in the refrigerator until needed. Briefly reheat them in boiling water just prior to combining with the soup. Lobster or shrimp can be used in place of the crab, and the morels may be swapped out for shiitake mushrooms.

serves **8**

1 tablespoon olive oil
1 cup finely chopped Vidalia onion
$1/2$ teaspoon kosher salt
1 cup cream sherry
1 pound potatoes, washed, peeled and
    chopped into 1-inch cubes
2 quarts low-sodium chicken broth
3 cups shelled spring peas
1 cup heavy cream
kosher salt to taste
1 cup (1-inch pieces) asparagus, blanched
    in boiling salted water
1 cup blanched shelled spring peas
$1/2$ cup morel mushroom halves, rinsed well
    and blanched in boiling salted water
    for $1/2$ minute
1 cup Maryland lump crab meat
2 tablespoons chopped chives
sour cream, truffle oil and/or fried julienned
    leeks, for garnish

Heat the olive oil in an 8-quart pot and stir in the onion. Add $1/2$ teaspoon salt and cook for 5 to 7 minutes over low to medium heat. Pour in the sherry and reduce until almost dry. Add the potatoes and chicken broth and simmer until the potatoes are tender, which should take 20 to 30 minutes.

Stir in 3 cups peas and the cream and simmer for an additional 5 minutes. Purée the mixture with an immersion blender. Adjust the seasoning with salt and keep warm. (If canned chicken broth is used, then no additional salt should be needed.)

Divide the asparagus, 1 cup blanched peas, mushrooms and crab meat among 8 soup bowls and pour the hot soup over the vegetables; sprinkle with the chives. Garnish with dollops of sour cream, a drizzle of fragrant white truffle oil and/or fried julienned leeks.

crab cocktail

This recipe is one of our most popular appetizers on the menu at Metro Bis. It combines a crab salad with a Bloody Mary and makes a great start to any meal or a fun beginning to a party. Made in minutes, it is refreshing and light and can be served in any season. I use pasteurized lump crab meat, but it also works well with cooked shrimp. Leftover vinaigrette and pickled onions can be stored in the refrigerator for up to two weeks.

serves 6

1 cup tomato juice
^{1}/2 cup horseradish
1 tablespoon Dijon mustard
^{1}/2 teaspoon black pepper
1 teaspoon sugar
^{1}/2 teaspoon celery salt
2 tablespoons lemon juice
1 tablespoon Worcestershire sauce
3 dashes Tabasco sauce
2 tablespoons olive oil
8 ounces Maryland lump crab meat
pickled onions
^{1}/4 cup (or more) vodka
katifi (shredded phyllo dough found frozen
    in Middle Eastern markets, baked
    and crumbled)

Combine the tomato juice, horseradish, Dijon mustard, pepper, sugar, celery salt, lemon juice, Worcestershire sauce, Tabasco sauce and olive oil in a medium bowl for the vinaigrette. This can also be done in a martini shaker and poured from it if you are looking to impress your friends.

Divide the crab meat evenly into 6 martini glasses. Place several pickled onion slices on top of the crab meat. Pour ^{1}/4 cup of the vinaigrette into each glass and add 1 tablespoon (or more) good-quality vodka to each glass. Garnish each with 2 tablespoons katifi.

Photograph for this recipe appears on page 113.

pickled onions
^{1}/2 cup thinly sliced onions
^{1}/4 cup white vinegar
pinch of sugar
pinch of kosher salt

Place the sliced onions in a shallow dish or bowl. Top with the vinegar, sugar and salt and let stand for 10 minutes.

According to his wife, Courtney Febbroriello, Prosperi is "Precision. Gliding hands. Dancing eyes. Controlled. Calm. Collected. Patient. Playfully daring with a dash of humor. The courage to dream and the motivation, persistence, and perseverance to capture it. The freedom of creation. He makes me potatoes with a smiling garnish. Two eyes of scallion, a tomato nose, and a carrot mouth."

spring pea sauce

Serve this delicious sauce with the oven-roasted trout with spring vegetable ragout or other spring entrées.

serves **6**

1 tablespoon butter
1 tablespoon chopped shallot, about 1 shallot
1 cup shelled peas
1/2 teaspoon kosher salt
1/4 cup good-quality extra-virgin olive oil
1/4 cup heavy cream

Heat a small saucepan over medium heat and add the butter and chopped shallot. Cook for 2 to 3 minutes. Toss in the peas and cook for 1 minute. Transfer to a blender and add the salt. Add the olive oil and cream slowly, processing constantly at medium speed. Taste and adjust the salt. Keep warm until ready to serve.

pear panna cotta
with pear william eau de vie

Panna cotta is my favorite dessert because it is a light alternative to a custard but still offers all the flavor and rich consistency one would expect from an after-dinner indulgence. Another benefit of panna cotta is that it should be made a day ahead of time, which frees up the cook to focus on dinner. It can also be made with numerous other fruits, including raspberries and strawberries.

serves **6**

2 cups milk
1 cup cream
1/2 cup sugar
pinch of salt
4 sheets gelatin
2 cups cold water
1/2 cup puréed poached pears or
    puréed canned pears
1/4 cup Pear William Eau de Vie
poached pears, for garnish

Combine the milk, cream, sugar and salt in a saucepan and simmer over low heat for 2 minutes; remove from the heat. Place the gelatin in a bowl with the cold water, covering the sheets completely. Let stand for 4 to 5 minutes or until the gelatin is soft and pliable; drain the water and squeeze the sheets dry.

Add the gelatin, pear purée and Pear William Eau de Vie to the milk mixture. Stir to incorporate all ingredients and dissolve the gelatin. Divide the mixture evenly into 6 molds or 6-ounce soup cups. Let sit in the refrigerator for 12 hours or until firm. Remove from the mold, garnish with poached pears and serve cold.

I never get angry when something comes out wrong. I just do it again. I've been working on pastrami for three years now. It never comes out exactly how I want it. There's still something missing...I like to keep six things going at once. I don't feel comfortable without everything going. As soon as one thing ends, I start something else.

yono**purnomo**

In 1971, flamboyant Chef Widjiono "Yono" Purnomo, a native of Jakarta, Indonesia, and graduate of Academy Perhotelan Negara in Bandung, Indonesia, embarked on a circuitous career journey in the dining rooms of the Holland America Cruise Lines.

He worked at fine table service, dining room management, and as a sommelier. He met his wife on the ship in 1996. After a shipboard romance, the pair married and settled in Albany, New York, where Yono found work in Albany's most elegant dining rooms. When the opportunity arose to open his own restaurant, Yono, a certified executive chef, "jumped ship" from the dining room to the kitchen and has never looked back.

In 1998, after thirteen years in a historic location, Yono joined forces with futurist and visionary Donald Metzner in breathing life into the one-of-a-kind Armory Center. The eponymous Yono's, now housed in an elegant two-story historic brownstone re-creation, features creative Continental fare highlighted with Indonesian specialties. Purnomo is also at the helm of Bumpers Café, an automotive-themed "eatertainment" venue, as well as a thriving banquet and catering operation.

In lieu of a formal culinary education, Yono has managed to learn from the industry's best in unorthodox ways, including winning apprenticeships on culinary Olympic teams. Yono credits Fritz Sonnenschmidt, culinary dean of the Culinary Institute of America in Hyde Park, New York, for instilling within him the credo, "Cook with your head, your heart, and your hands," and always be willing to share your expertise.

Chef Purnomo has represented New York State in the American Seafood Challenge, a prestigious national competition held in New Orleans, has been featured on television shows, and has presented his cuisine to sold-out audiences at Manhattan's famed James Beard House three times. Yono's menu has been replicated for 7,000 of Cornell University's students and faculty through their Cross Country Gourmet program. He was selected as a member of the National Chefs Touring Program for the Indonesian Festival and was recently featured as one of twenty-eight guest chefs at the Eighth Annual James Beard Awards reception Flavors of the Far East, an Asian extravaganza for 1,200 guests.

Photographer
steve**caparulo**

Food Stylist
vicki**caparulo**

Cook with your head, your heart, and your hands.

rack of **lamb**

y p

recipesrecipes

Rack of Lamb in Indonesian Curry Sauce

Warm Spiced Bananas

rack of lamb in indonesian curry sauce

serves **8**

1/2 cup olive oil
1/2 tablespoon chopped shallots
1/2 tablespoon chopped garlic
1/2 teaspoon coriander

1/2 teaspoon cumin
1/2 teaspoon chopped fresh basil
8 (12- to 14-ounce) racks of lamb
Indonesian curry sauce

Combine the olive oil, shallots, garlic, coriander, cumin and basil in a large bowl. Add the racks of lamb and mix to coat well. Marinate for at least 1 hour.

Chargrill or broil the marinated racks of lamb to your preferred temperature (I suggest rare). Allow the meat to rest for 3 to 4 minutes before slicing. Place a pool of the Indonesian curry sauce on a plate and fan the chops atop the sauce. Wonderful with grilled vegetables.

indonesian curry sauce

1/2 tablespoon coriander
1/2 tablespoon cumin
1 teaspoon turmeric
2 tablespoons curry powder
2 to 3 tablespoons water
2 tablespoons chopped shallots
1 tablespoon chopped garlic
2 teaspoons sambal
1 tablespoon tamarind paste
1 stalk lemon grass, pounded

2 tablespoons thinly sliced Laos ginger (galangal)
1/2 cup coconut milk
vegetable oil
1 1/2 cups coconut milk
10 kaffir lime leaves
1 cup mango chutney
4 cloves
1 cinnamon stick
1/2 tablespoon sambal oelek (freshly ground chili paste available in Asian markets)

Combine the coriander, cumin, turmeric and curry powder with the water in a bowl and pound to form a paste. Set aside.

Process the shallots, garlic, sambal, tamarind paste, lemon grass, ginger and 1/2 cup coconut milk in a food processor. This will form a smooth paste known in Indonesian cooking as bumbu.

Sauté the bumbu paste in hot oil in a sauté pan for about 3 or 4 minutes, stirring constantly. Add 1 1/2 cups coconut milk, the kaffir leaves, mango chutney, cloves, cinnamon stick and sambal oelek. Continue cooking to a simmer.

Allow to cool slightly, then strain. Return to the heat and continue to simmer until the sauce coats the back of a spoon.

Though I began my career in the food service industry in the front of the house aboard Holland America Line's flagship, the MS Rotterdam, I found that my true passion was behind the stove. I am a native of Indonesia, which is rich in culture, art, history, and cuisine. It has been my profound pleasure to share the culture and cuisine of my native land for the past twenty-five years here in America. I'm amazed at how much the culinary scene has changed in America. When I opened my first restaurant, it was nearly impossible to get the ingredients to create authentic ethnic cuisine. Now these items have become staples in supermarkets.

warm spiced bananas

serves 8

1/2 cup (1 stick) butter

4 ounces palm sugar

1/4 cup (2 ounces) banana liqueur

1/4 cup (2 ounces) Grand Marnier

1/2 cup fresh orange juice

juice of 1 lime

3 pandan leaves, tied in knots (available in Asian markets; it looks like scallion but imparts a wonderful vanilla-malt flavor)

1 cup coconut milk

8 ripe bananas, peeled and bias-sliced to yield 4 slices per banana

1 pint premium vanilla ice cream

heavy cream, whipped, for garnish

Heat a 12-inch sauté pan over medium heat. Add the butter and palm sugar and melt together until smooth. Deglaze and flame with the banana liqueur and Grand Marnier. Add the orange juice and lime juice, stirring to combine. Place the knotted pandan leaves in the pan. Add the coconut milk and bring to a simmer. Add the bananas to the sauté pan and cook until fork-tender.

Remove the knotted pandan leaves; they are for flavoring only. Place a scoop of the ice cream on each plate. Fan out the bananas on the plates and spoon the sauce over the ice cream and bananas. Garnish with fresh whipped cream if desired.

charlesramseyer

Charles Ramseyer was named one of five of America's Most Inventive Fish Chefs by the *Wine Spectator* in March of 2004. Charles discovered his love of the kitchen as a teenager and soon afterward became an apprentice at the exclusive Hotel Vorderen Sternen in Zurich.

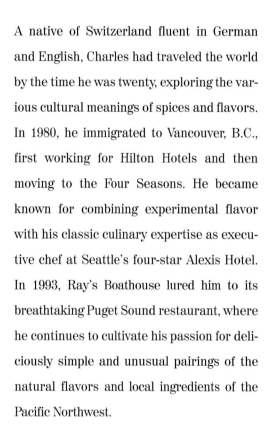

A native of Switzerland fluent in German and English, Charles had traveled the world by the time he was twenty, exploring the various cultural meanings of spices and flavors. In 1980, he immigrated to Vancouver, B.C., first working for Hilton Hotels and then moving to the Four Seasons. He became known for combining experimental flavor with his classic culinary expertise as executive chef at Seattle's four-star Alexis Hotel. In 1993, Ray's Boathouse lured him to its breathtaking Puget Sound restaurant, where he continues to cultivate his passion for deliciously simple and unusual pairings of the natural flavors and local ingredients of the Pacific Northwest.

In 1997, Charles was invited to prepare a succulent Dungeness crab feast as part of the prestigious James Beard Foundation's Special Event Series. He appeared at the James Beard House again in 2002 and was a guest instructor at the prestigious French Culinary Institute in New York City. He made a second trip to New York to help accept the James Beard Foundation 2002 Bertolli Olive Oil America's Classic Award presented to longstanding, locally owned and operated regional restaurants that are beloved by their communities. Since then, Charles has been invited to act as guest chef for numerous hotels and events, including the Hilton Beijing, the 2003 International Taste Washington tour to Tokyo sponsored by the Washington Wine Commission, and the 2003 James Beard Foundation Awards Gala. In addition, Charles gives generously of his time to the community.

Much of last year was also devoted to the cookbook titled *Ray's Boathouse: Seafood Secrets of the Pacific Northwest*, which was released in April 2003. "We really tried to make the recipes user-friendly," says Charles, who has served as Ray's executive chef for the past twelve years. The cookbook coincided with Ray's thirtieth anniversary and is available nationwide.

Photographer
johnsherlock

Food Stylist
nathanfong

I became particularly intrigued with "East meets West."

cumin-rubbed sturgeon

recipesrecipes

Cumin-Rubbed Sturgeon with Heirloom Tomato Vinaigrette and

  Black Lentil Chanterelle Ragout

Pacific Oysters on a Spoon

Smoked Tomato Soup with Basil Oil and Parmesan Crisps

Yakima Peach and Blackberry Crisp with Caramel Sauce

4 (7-ounce) sturgeon fillets,
  skin removed

1/4 cup cumin rub

2 tablespoons olive oil

heirloom tomato vinaigrette

black lentil chanterelle ragout

1/2 cup chevron-cut green
  onions

cumin-rubbed sturgeon
with heirloom tomato vinaigrette and
black lentil chanterelle ragout

Preheat the oven to 400 degrees. Dredge the flesh side of the fillets in the cumin rub. Heat the olive oil in a large ovenproof nonstick skillet over medium-high heat just until smoking. Place the fillets spiced side down in the pan and sear until browned, about 1 to 2 minutes, being careful not to scorch the spices, which will make them bitter. Turn the fillets over and place the pan in the oven. Roast until the flesh is firm to the touch and just cooked through, about 5 minutes.

Spoon a pool of heirloom tomato vinaigrette in the centers of 4 plates. Mound the black lentil chanterelle ragout in the vinaigrette. Drape the sturgeon over the ragout, spiced side up. Sprinkle with the green onions. Serve immediately.

cumin rub

1 tablespoon ground cumin

1 tablespoon granulated garlic

1 teaspoon Madras curry powder

2 teaspoons celery salt

1/2 teaspoon ground black pepper

1/4 teaspoon kosher salt

1/2 teaspoon sugar

Mix the cumin, garlic, curry powder, celery salt, pepper, salt and sugar in a bowl. Reserve 2 teaspoons cumin rub for the black lentil chanterelle ragout.

heirloom tomato vinaigrette

1 Marvel Stripe heirloom tomato, chopped

1 tablespoon chopped shallot

1/2 cup seasoned rice wine vinegar

1/2 cup water

1 teaspoon Dijon mustard

1 cup canola oil

kosher salt

freshly ground black pepper

Purée the tomato, shallot, vinegar, water and mustard in a blender. Add the canola oil in a slow steady stream, blending constantly. Season with salt and pepper to taste.

black lentil chanterelle ragout

2 tablespoons olive oil

1 tablespoon minced garlic

1/2 cup chopped leeks

1/2 cup chopped celery

1 cup chopped carrots

1/2 cup chopped fennel

1 cup uncooked black lentils

2 teaspoons cumin rub

4 cups vegetable stock

8 ounces chanterelle mushrooms, sliced

1/2 teaspoon granulated garlic

1/2 teaspoon fresh thyme

1/2 teaspoon kosher salt

1/4 teaspoon ground black pepper

1 tablespoon olive oil

Heat 2 tablespoons olive oil in a medium saucepan over medium heat. Add the minced garlic and cook, stirring, until the garlic begins to brown. Add the leeks, celery, carrots and fennel and sauté until the vegetables begin to soften, about 3 to 4 minutes. Add the lentils and stir to mix. Add the cumin rub and stir. Add the vegetable stock and bring to a simmer. Simmer gently until the lentils are tender, about 30 minutes.

Preheat the oven to 350 degrees. Combine the mushrooms, granulated garlic, thyme, salt and pepper in a bowl. Drizzle with 1 tablespoon olive oil and mix well to coat. Spread the mushrooms on a sheet pan lined with parchment paper. Roast until the mushrooms begin to dry out and become a little crunchy, about 10 to 15 minutes, being careful not to burn. Fold into the cooked lentils.

pacific oysters on a spoon

serves **4 to 6**

24 medium-sized fresh Pacific oysters in
    the shell, or 1 jar extra-small shucked
    Pacific oysters
1/2 cup dry sauvignon blanc
1/2 cup fish stock or water
24 Chinese ceramic soup spoons
1/2 cup heavy cream
kosher salt
freshly ground black pepper
2 tablespoons chopped chives or parsley,
    or 1 tablespoon tobiko caviar, for garnish

Shuck the oysters, saving the oyster liquor, and place in a bowl; discard the shells. Trim the abductor muscle with scissors if desired.

Bring the wine and fish stock to a boil in a 2½-quart saucepan. Drop in the oysters and their liquor and poach until the oysters become plump and opaque, about 1 minute. Remove the oysters from the pot, place in the spoons, and keep warm.

Reduce the liquid remaining in the saucepan over medium-high heat by half. Add the cream and bring the mixture back to a boil. Reduce the mixture until thick and syrupy, about 5 minutes. Season the sauce with salt and pepper to taste and spoon over the oysters in the spoons. Garnish with chives, parsley or caviar. Serve immediately.

I began my lifelong passion for food cooking at my mother's side at age eight. By the time I was a teenager, I was putting on cooking classes for my peers. By age twenty-one, I became particularly intrigued with the "East meets West" style of cuisine and took off on a world adventure, exploring the foods of Singapore, Hong Kong, Beijing, Tokyo, and Bangkok, working in hotels and restaurants along the way. I arrived in Seattle by way of Vancouver through four-star hotels and found a home at Ray's Boathouse in 1992. Ray's allows me the freedom to explore my culinary creativity using the finest northwestern ingredients with a modern Asian-Western flair.

smoked tomato soup
with basil oil and parmesan crisps

12 Roma tomatoes

3 tablespoons olive oil

1 tablespoon minced garlic

3/4 cup chopped carrots

1/2 cup chopped celery

1/2 cup chopped onion

1/3 cup all-purpose flour

4 cups vegetable stock
  or water

1 tablespoon tomato paste

2 tablespoons dry sherry

2 teaspoons ancho chile
  powder

1 teaspoon smoked paprika

1 tablespoon packed light
  brown sugar

1 teaspoon dried thyme

kosher salt to taste

ground white pepper to taste

basil oil

parmesan crisps

Prepare a smoker using applewood chips. Trim the stem ends of the tomatoes and cut into halves lengthwise through the core; place cut side up on a rack in the smoker. Hot-smoke until the tomatoes are darkened and slightly wilted, about 30 to 40 minutes. Remove, cool, and pull the skins off the tomatoes. These can be made a day in advance and refrigerated.

Heat the olive oil in a 5-quart stockpot over medium-high heat. Add the garlic and sauté until browned, about 1 minute. Add the carrots, celery and onion. Cook, stirring frequently, until the vegetables begin to soften, about 5 minutes. Reduce the heat to medium and add the flour, stirring to mix well. Stir in the smoked tomatoes and vegetable stock.

Bring the soup to a boil, then reduce the heat to a simmer. Add the tomato paste, sherry, ancho chile powder, paprika, brown sugar, thyme, salt and white pepper. Simmer, stirring occasionally, until the vegetables are tender, about 25 minutes. Purée with a handheld blender or food processor until smooth. This can be made a day in advance and reheated.

Ladle the soup into serving bowls, drizzle with basil oil and serve with parmesan crisps.

parmesan crisps
1 cup (4 ounces) finely grated Parmesan cheese

Preheat the oven to 350 degrees. Line a baking sheet with parchment paper and grease generously with olive oil or cooking spray (or use a nonstick baking sheet or a nonstick bakeware liner, such as Silpat).

Sprinkle the cheese into 4 ovals in a thin, lacy layer, not a thick pile. Bake until the cheese is golden and bubbling, about 15 minutes. Remove from the oven and, while they are still hot and pliable, carefully remove the crisps from the baking sheet and drape over a rolling pin or wine bottle to shape them into a curve. Cool completely. These can be made a few hours in advance and stored at room temperature.

basil oil
1 teaspoon kosher salt
1 cup packed fresh basil leaves
1 cup canola oil
pinch of kosher salt

Fill a 2-quart pot 3/4 full with water and add 1 teaspoon salt. Bring the water to a rolling boil. Drop in the basil leaves and stir for 10 seconds. Drain the water through a strainer and immediately place the blanched basil under cold running water. When cool, squeeze out the excess water.

Combine the blanched basil, canola oil and pinch of salt in a blender or food processor. Process until well combined, about 4 to 5 minutes. Transfer to a condiment squeeze bottle. This can be made a day in advance and refrigerated. Shake well before using.

yakima peach and blackberry crisp
with caramel sauce

serves **6 to 8**

2 tablespoons cornstarch
$1/4$ teaspoon cinnamon
$1/8$ teaspoon salt
$1/8$ teaspoon nutmeg
2 tablespoons cold water
2 pounds fresh Yakima peaches, sliced,
    about 8 cups
6 tablespoons sugar
2 cups blackberries
$1/2$ cup all-purpose flour
$1/4$ cup packed light brown sugar
$1/4$ cup oats
$1/4$ cup chopped walnuts
$1/4$ teaspoon cinnamon
pinch of salt
$2^1/2$ tablespoons unsalted butter, softened
vanilla bean ice cream
caramel sauce

Preheat the oven to 400 degrees. Combine the cornstarch, $1/4$ teaspoon cinnamon, $1/8$ teaspoon salt, nutmeg and water in a small bowl and whisk until smooth; set aside.

Combine the peaches and sugar in a large saucepan. Cook over medium-high heat, stirring frequently, until the peaches are tender and the liquid from the sugar and peaches begins to boil; if the peaches are very ripe, the cooking time will be minimal. Remove the pan from the heat and add the cornstarch mixture. Cook, stirring constantly, until the filling begins to thicken. If it does not thicken, cook over medium heat for a few minutes longer, stirring constantly. Remove from the heat and gently fold in the blackberries. Spoon into six 8-ounce ovenproof bowls or ramekins or an $8^1/2 \times 11$-inch baking pan.

Combine the flour, brown sugar, oats, walnuts, $1/4$ teaspoon cinnamon and a pinch of salt in the bowl of an electric mixer fitted with a paddle attachment. Add the butter and mix until completely blended. Spoon a thin layer over the filling to cover completely. Bake on the top oven rack until the topping is golden brown and the filling is bubbling, about 15 to 20 minutes. Serve warm with vanilla bean ice cream and caramel sauce.

caramel sauce
$1^1/2$ cups sugar
$1^3/4$ teaspoons lemon juice
1 pint heavy cream
$1/4$ cup ($1/2$ stick) unsalted butter

Combine the sugar and lemon juice in a medium saucepan over medium-high heat and cook, swirling the pan as the sugar melts to prevent scorching. Continue to cook and swirl until the sugar is completely melted and turns a dark amber color; protect your hands with oven mitts or pot holders.

Whisk the cream slowly into the melted sugar in the pan. Stir any large pieces of sugar back into the caramel over low heat until remelted. Bring the sauce to a boil, reduce the heat to medium and cook, without stirring, for 5 minutes. Remove from the heat and immediately stir in the butter. Refrigerate until ready to use.

miguel**ravago**

Chef Miguel Ravago's passion for food is a legacy of his Mexican culinary traditions. The heirloom recipes bequeathed to him by his mother, Amelia Velasquez Ravago, and his grandmother, Guadalupe Velasquez, are the foundation of his cooking repertoire to this day.

In 1972, Miguel's home cooking was part of what motivated his friend Tom Gilliland to open their first restaurant, the San Angel Inn, in Houston. By 1975, the pair had moved to Austin and founded Fonda San Miguel, maybe the first restaurant in the United States to feature an entire menu of authentic dishes from the interior of Mexico.

...commitment to the foods of his heritage

In the beginning, it wasn't clear whether it was courage or folly that prompted the pair to open a one-of-a-kind eatery in an area where Tex-Mex was well established and popular. For starters, many of the necessary ingredients, such as fresh and dried chiles, nopales, tomatillos, and black beans, were almost impossible to find locally and had to be imported directly from Mexico. But Miguel's commitment to the foods of his heritage,

along with mentoring and consultation from the doyenne of Mexican food, Diana Kennedy, ensured that Fonda San Miguel would develop a loyal following.

As the restaurant approaches its thirtieth anniversary, staple ingredients for Mexican foods are much more common in many areas of the country. These days, Miguel's passion extends to procuring the finest quality of raw materials for his restaurant kitchen. He insists on Niman Ranch beef and pork and Jamison Farms lamb and is scouting organic Mexican corn to make his own masa for fresh corn tortillas. If you're in Austin, drop into Fonda San Miguel for brunch some Sunday and find Miguel indulging in one of his greatest pleasures—standing at the brunch buffet describing the rich culinary history of the dishes he presents to his satisfied clientele.

Photographer
irisrichardson

Food Stylist
roberta**rall**

jicama salad

recipesrecipes

Jicama Salad

Chipotle Potato Gratin

Borrego Lamb Chops

miguel**ravago** 129

jicama salad

This refreshing salad comes from the Mexican state of Jalisco, where it is known as pico de gallo, or rooster's beak. I have found it is equally good made with Rio Star grapefruit, pineapple, blood oranges, cantaloupe, watermelon, and honeydew. The contrast of sweet fruit, crunchy jicama, tangy lime juice, and a little dash of chili powder makes for a delightful palate cleanser. It is a popular item on the Sunday buffet.

serves 6

1 large jicama, peeled and cut into matchsticks
2 navel oranges, peeled and sectioned with
    no white pulp
1/2 large cantaloupe, cut into bite-size pieces
1/2 large honeydew melon, cut into
    bite-size pieces
1/2 cup pomegranate seeds, if in season
1 cup fresh lime juice
2 sprigs fresh cilantro, chopped
1 teaspoon salt
1/2 teaspoon chili powder (optional)

Combine the jicama, oranges, cantaloupe, honeydew melon and pomegranate seeds in a nonreactive bowl. Add the lime juice, cilantro and salt and toss to mix well. Chill for about 1 hour for the flavors to blend. Toss with the chili powder before serving.

chipotle potato gratin

serves 6 to 8

2 pounds Yukon Gold potatoes or large red
    potatoes, peeled and thinly sliced
1 teaspoon salt
1 1/4 cups crème fraîche or heavy cream
2 small garlic cloves, minced
2 or 3 canned chipotle chiles in adobo sauce,
    including a little of the sauce
2 cups (8 ounces) shredded manchego cheese
2 tablespoons chopped chives

Preheat the oven to 350 degrees. Butter a 9×9-inch glass or ceramic baking dish. Combine the potatoes and salt in a 3-quart saucepan and cover with water. Bring to a boil and boil for 6 minutes; drain.

Combine the crème fraîche, garlic and chipotle chiles in a blender and purée. Arrange half the potatoes in the prepared baking dish. Pour half the cream mixture evenly over the potatoes and sprinkle with half the cheese. Repeat the layers and sprinkle with the chives.

Cover with foil and bake for 30 minutes or until tender. Increase the oven temperature to 400 degrees. Uncover the potatoes and bake for 30 minutes longer or until the top is golden brown. Let stand for 15 minutes before serving. Serve warm.

borrego lamb chops

Fonda San Miguel owner Tom Gilliland is an ardent supporter of the Slow Food movement. He is a stickler for serving only the best quality ingredients available to customers at Fonda San Miguel. The meat for these delicious lamb chops comes from Jamison Farms in Latrobe, Pennsylvania. The lamb is grass-fed and free of hormones, pesticides, and antibiotics. I serve this dish with a chipotle potato gratin and a mixed green salad. The spice rub is good for lamb chops, pork chops, or steak, and it is also great on corn on the cob.

serves **12**

1/4 cup corn oil
7 whole chipotle chiles, seeded and deveined
2 whole ancho chiles, seeded and deveined
12 garlic cloves
3/4 cup kosher salt
1/4 cup dried Mexican oregano, toasted
24 (2 1/2-ounce) lamb rib chops
olive oil
chipotle potato gratin (page 130)

Heat the corn oil in a heavy skillet over medium-high heat until hot, but not smoking. Add the chiles 1 or 2 at a time and fry until they puff up and brown, about 10 seconds each; do not allow them to burn or the rub will be bitter. Drain the chiles on paper towels to cool and crisp; you can discard the oil or save in a jar to flavor soups, stews and sauces. Grind the chiles to a fine powder in a spice grinder.

Combine the ground chiles with the garlic, salt and toasted oregano in a food processor and process to a salt-like consistency. If the mixture seems wet, spread it in an even layer on a baking sheet and dry in a 150-degree oven for 1 hour or until no longer moist, breaking up any lumps with the fingers. Store in a covered container and regrind before using after storing.

Heat a grill to medium-hot. Rub the lamb chops with olive oil and a generous portion of the spice rub mixture. Place the chops fat side down on the grill and grill for 2 to 3 minutes or until brown. Reduce the heat to medium and move the chops to the upper level of the grill. Cook on the bone side for 8 to 10 minutes longer for medium. Serve with the chipotle potato gratin or rice and a salad.

john**shields**

John Shields is a nationally acclaimed expert in regional American coastal cuisine. His career began informally when, at a very early age, he worked with his grandmother, Gertie Cleary, in a church hall kitchen. Grandmom Gertie was the perfect teacher.

His professional career began by accident. After studying at the Peabody Conservatory of Music, this Baltimore native moved to Cape Cod with aspirations of becoming a rock star and played the piano in bars. Then, one day, an injured friend asked John to work his shift in the kitchen of a popular Cape Cod inn. Little did John know that his first day, spent making thirty-six pie shells, would evolve into many years as a chef, restaurant owner, author, and host of a food television program.

In the 1980s, John moved to northern California, where he joined the New American Food revolution. He was first executive chef of A La Carte in Berkeley. But he missed the food of his youth, so he opened his own restaurant, named it for his grandmother, and began to introduce San Francisco Bay residents to the wonderful regional American fare of the Chesapeake Bay. *California* magazine soon hailed Gertie's as "a shining star in the culinary constellation of northern California restaurants."

Nearly two decades and many, many crab cakes later, John made his way back to Baltimore, where he now lives. He owns and operates an award-winning restaurant, Gertrude's, at the Baltimore Museum of Art —still paying homage to his grandmother, though a little more formally. John is the author of several cookbooks on the cuisine of Chesapeake Bay, and, in 1998, public television stations across the country began airing John's series, *Chesapeake Bay Cooking*, featuring local folks and their dishes. Recently, he has begun to tape his new public television series.

His writing has appeared in many national and regional publications, and he is a frequent guest chef on radio and television and teaches classes on American coastal cooking at private culinary arts institutions around the country.

And, by the way, he still wants to be a rock star.

Photographer
michaelbrennan

Food Stylist
judymentzer

my's green **papaya salad**

• *Grandmom Gertie was the perfect teacher.*

j
•

recipesrecipes

My's Green Papaya Salad

Eastern Shore Cantaloupe Soup

js

my's green papaya salad

My is not me. My is My Phuong. She is my West Coast sister, daughter of longtime friend and mentor, Lan Huynh, also known as Mama Lan. Mama was a brilliant cook, and in this case, as the saying goes, the papaya did not fall far from the tree. My prepares this exceptionally refreshing salad with grated papaya that is dressed with a fiery and sweet citrus dressing. It may be served as a first course or as an entrée.

serves 2

1 large green papaya, about 7 to 8 inches long, peeled, seeded and thinly shredded
spicy fish sauce
4 large steamed shrimp, peeled, deveined and cut into halves lengthwise
2 ounces boiled pork loin, thinly sliced
3 tablespoons peanuts, coarsely chopped
8 mint leaves, julienned

Mix the shredded papaya with the spicy fish sauce in a bowl and divide into 2 bowls. Top with equal portions of the shrimp, pork, peanuts and mint leaves.

spicy fish sauce

3 garlic cloves, finely minced
3 Thai chiles, finely minced (see note)
3 tablespoons lime juice
2 tablespoons sugar
1 lime, sectioned, seeded and chopped
3 tablespoons fish sauce (nam pla)

Mix the garlic, chiles, lime juice, sugar and lime segments in a small bowl. Add the fish sauce and mix thoroughly. If the sauce is too thick, thin with a little water.

Note: Wear gloves when handling chiles, and don't allow them to touch the bare skin. If you can't find Thai chiles, use jalapeños, serranos or 1 tablespoon sambal, a Thai chile sauce that can be found in Asian markets or gourmet specialty shops.

Normally during hot months at the Eastern Shore, my appetite somewhat wanes, and I crave lighter fare. My's Green Papaya Salad fits the bill with crisp, brightly flavored papaya tossed with shrimp, pork, toasted peanuts, and a spicy fish sauce scented with mint and lime. To wrap up this refreshing repast, bananas are bathed in a sesame-coconut cream, packaged in paper-thin egg roll wrappers, lightly fried, and served warm, hopefully with homemade vanilla ice cream. This is a table overflowing with memories of wonderful times and the aromas and tastes prepared for me by my Gertie and Lan—my culinary mothers.

eastern shore **cantaloupe soup**

This light, refreshing soup is reminiscent of summertime dinners held on the screened porch during the hot Chesapeake summers. My grandmother, Gertie Cleary, and many of her friends on the eastern shore of the Chesapeake Bay, made versions of this soup every summer, when the melons are at their sweetest. Her girlfriends would come over for afternoon luncheons, and this chilled soup was a refreshing favorite on those rather humid summer days. We prepare this soup often in the warm months at my restaurant, Gertrude's (sound familiar?), and drizzle a little fresh berry purée on top just before serving. This recipe also works beautifully with other ripe melons, such as honeydew.

serves **8**

4 ripe cantaloupes
1 fifth dry Champagne
1/2 cup freshly chopped mint
lemon twists or mint sprigs, for garnish
fresh berry sauce (optional)

Peel and seed 3 of the cantaloupes and cut into pieces. Purée the cantaloupe in batches in a blender, adding Champagne to each batch to thin to a thickish soup consistency. Chill well before serving.

Cut the remaining melon in half, discard the seeds and scoop out the flesh with a melon baller. Add these melon balls to the soup along with the chopped mint. Serve in chilled bowls with a lemon twist or mint sprig and a drizzle of berry sauce.

fresh berry sauce

2 pints fresh raspberries or strawberries
1/2 cup sugar dissolved in 1/2 cup hot water
2 tablespoons freshly squeezed lemon juice

Purée the berries in a blender. Pour in the sugar water and lemon juice with the blender running and process until quite smooth. Put the purée through a sieve if necessary to remove the seeds. Store in the refrigerator for several days.

I remember, as a small boy in Baltimore, my grandmother's excitement with each approaching season and the treasures it offered for the table. We would marvel at the first asparagus of the spring, breathe in the sweet, musky fragrance of ripe Eastern Shore melons, and laugh at the antics of feisty blue crabs as they escaped from overflowing bushel baskets. When my grandmother prepared the food, be it vine-ripened tomatoes or fresh-from-the-bay rockfish, I was always aware of the quiet reverence she felt for these prized gifts.

shelley**sikora**

Shelley Sikora is co-owner with her husband, Bob, of Bobby McGee's restaurant in Phoenix, Arizona. She once ran the Bobby McGee's chain of twenty-four full-service restaurants in eight states.

Among many of their successful concepts is Juice Works, a smoothies franchise that they eventually sold to TCBY. Shelley's first published cookbook, *An Italian Affair*, was released in December 2002. The book is a tribute to her mother, who was a professional chef and baker specializing in desserts and pastries. With this book, Shelley combines elements of traditional Italian cooking with regional Sicilian characteristics, all finished with the simplicity and speed that today's home chef demands.

Shelley has written another cookbook to be released in spring 2005. She also finds time to teach cooking classes, host a television show, *Home Plates*, and appear on local TV and radio.

...combines elements of traditional Italian cooking with regional Sicilian characteristics...

Photographer
ken**epstein**

Food Stylist
debbie**elder**

tomarella tart

recipesrecipes

Cracklin' Basil Tomarella Tarts

Ricotta Beignets

Savory Veal with Lemon and Sage Sauce and Polenta with Mascarpone

shelley**sikora** 137

cracklin' basil tomarella tarts

Use different colors of heirloom tomatoes if you can find them for these colorful tarts.

serves 12

1 package frozen puff pastry, thawed
1 (12-ounce) jar sun-dried tomato pesto
4 large ripe tomatoes, thinly sliced
1 bunch fresh basil
2 cups canola oil
12 bocconcini mozzarella balls

Preheat the oven to 475 degrees. Use 1 sheet of puff pastry at a time to cut four 6-inch rounds. Repeat to produce 12 rounds. Place the pastry rounds on a lightly greased baking sheet and brush with the tomato pesto. Top with the fresh tomato slices. Bake for 20 minutes or until the pastry is golden brown; cool.

Wash the basil leaves, cut off the stems and pinch off a little more than 12 large leaves. Heat the canola oil in a medium sauté pan. Add the basil leaves and sauté for 2 to 3 seconds; remove and place carefully on a paper towel. Place a mozzarella ball on each tart and top with a cracklin' basil leaf. Serve on individual plates.

ricotta beignets

makes 2 dozen

vegetable oil for deep-frying
6 eggs
1/2 cup sugar
1 pound ricotta cheese
1 1/2 cups cake flour
1 (heaping) tablespoon baking powder
1 teaspoon vanilla extract
1/4 cup finely chopped almonds
confectioners' sugar
ice cream or gelato
chocolate syrup

Pour enough vegetable oil into a deep saucepan to reach halfway up the side. Heat the oil to 350 to 365 degrees. Mix the eggs, sugar, ricotta cheese, cake flour, baking powder, vanilla and almonds in the order listed with a wooden spoon in a bowl until smooth.

Use a melon ball scoop to scoop out the batter, then push it off into the hot oil; the batter will sink, then float to the top of the oil. Deep-fry, turning occasionally to fry evenly on all sides.

Drain on paper towels and roll in confectioners' sugar. Serve immediately with a scoop of your favorite ice cream or gelato and drizzle with chocolate syrup.

savory veal with lemon and sage sauce and polenta with mascarpone

serves **8 to 10**

2¹/2 pounds thinly sliced veal scaloppine
kosher salt to taste
freshly ground black pepper to taste
all-purpose flour
¹/4 cup extra-virgin olive oil
1¹/2 cups dry white wine
4 cups chicken broth
2 cups beef broth
¹/4 cup chopped fresh sage
4 teaspoons lemon peel
¹/2 cup (1 stick) butter, chilled and cut into pieces
polenta with mascarpone

Season the veal with salt and pepper. Coat with flour, shaking off the excess. Heat the olive oil in a heavy large skillet over high heat. Add the veal to the skillet in batches and fry until brown, about 2 minutes per side. Transfer the veal to a platter. Tent with foil and discard the oil from the skillet.

Add the wine to the same skillet and bring to a boil. Boil for 3 minutes, stirring to deglaze the skillet. Add the chicken broth, beef broth, sage and lemon peel. Bring to a boil, then reduce the heat and simmer until reduced to 1 cup, about 15 minutes. Remove from the heat and whisk in the butter just until melted. Season with salt and pepper.

Place the veal on a platter and top with the sauce. Serve with the polenta.

polenta with mascarpone

10 cups water
2 cups quick-cooking yellow or white polenta
2 cups mascarpone cheese

Bring the water to a boil in a large saucepan. Add the polenta in a thin stream, whisking constantly until all is incorporated. Cook until the polenta is as thick and dense as cream of wheat, stirring constantly. Spoon the polenta into warmed serving bowls and top each with ¹/4 cup of the mascarpone cheese.

allen**susser**

The *New York Times* called Allen Susser the "Ponce de León of New Florida cooking." He established Chef Allen's restaurant in 1986, and it remains a Miami area favorite. His new Palm Tree Cuisine is fresh and flavorful, like a tropical vacation on a plate.

After earning degrees from New York City Tech, Florida International University, and the Cordon Bleu, he worked at the Bristol Hotel in Paris and went on to cook in fabled kitchens of Florida and New York, most notably that of Le Cirque.

Chef Allen's cross-cultural, tropical cuisine started with New World cuisine more than fifteen years ago and has been constantly evolving. His vision of what the future holds is a culinary fusion of cultures that share similar landscapes and tropical ingredients.

Food is my life, my profession, my charity, and my diversion.

The cuisines derived from the Caribbean, Latin America, the Pacific Rim, and the tropical Mediterranean are ideal for fusion in a sweet, spicy, and aromatic harmony. They all fit together very well, though each offers a diverse spice box full of exotic flavors.

In May 1994, Allen received the James Beard Foundation's Award for Best Chef: Southeast region. During 1995, he was granted an honorary doctorate from Johnson and Wales University. Also in 1995, he had his first book published—*New World Cuisine and Cookery*—followed two years later by *The Great Citrus Book* and his latest release, *The Great Mango Book*.

Other honors include the Torch Award for Leadership from Florida International University; the prestigious Best Chef award from the James Beard Foundation; *Gourmet* magazine Top Table Award in South Florida; and Best Restaurant for Food in Miami from the *Zagat Survey*. He serves on the National Board of Directors for the American Institute of Wine and Food. In addition to appearing in national publications, Allen has also appeared on several television programs. He consults for American Airlines, KitchenAid, McCormick Spice, and Sunkist.

Photographer
jimscherzi

Food Stylist
davidlenweaver

pan-fried **red snapper**

recipesrecipes

Pan-Fried Red Snapper with Spicy Mango Glaze

Mango Mojito

Mango and Crab Salad

Handmade Mango Pastel

pan-fried red snapper
with spicy mango glaze

This is a simple recipe with a powerful flavor. The glaze calls for very ripe mangoes. Nothing prepared me for the experience of mangoes that greeted me in Miami. The whole neighborhood possesses this deep ambrosial fragrance in mango season. The varieties of mango exceed anything I could have imagined, and I have been on a quest to sample as many kinds of mango as I can. We have 150 kinds just in this region.

serves **4**

1/3 cup red wine vinegar
1/4 cup packed brown sugar
1/4 teaspoon ground cumin
1/2 teaspoon kosher salt
1 teaspoon finely chopped jalapeño pepper
1 teaspoon finely chopped fresh ginger
1/2 cup fresh mango purée
2 tablespoons olive oil
4 (6-ounce) red snapper fillets
1 teaspoon kosher salt
1/2 teaspoon freshly ground black pepper
8 fresh cilantro sprigs, for garnish

Combine the vinegar, brown sugar, cumin, 1/2 teaspoon salt, jalapeño pepper and ginger in a small saucepan. Bring to a boil and simmer for 3 minutes or until caramelized. Mix in the mango purée and simmer for another minute.

Heat the olive oil in a heavy-bottomed sauté pan until it begins to smoke. Season the fillets with 1 teaspoon salt and the pepper. Cook in the oil for 2 to 3 minutes on each side or until crisp. Brush the mango glaze on the fish and continue to cook for 2 more minutes. Remove from the pan and set aside on a warm plate. Garnish with the fresh cilantro sprigs.

When I first opened my restaurant, I placed a small ad in the local newspaper, "I will trade dinner for mangoes. Bring me your backyard fruit," and it listed my phone number. Each summer, I have almost more fruit than I can use.

We use the fruit in every possible way: I make mango martinis, mango mojitos, mango upside-down cake, mango tarte Tatin with ginger, mango chutney, mango ketchup. I stew them, grate them when they're still green, grill them, use them in curries and salsas and ice creams. I simply can't exhaust the possibilities; mangoes are our community fruit.

Sometimes we do get so many at one time that we donate mangoes to a local food bank. In 2004, 3,000 pounds of mangoes came to our kitchen door. I didn't purchase mangoes for four months. And in exchange, we create a full-course dinner for each couple that brings us mangoes, using them hard and green or firm and tart or sweet and melting in the dishes we serve them.

mango mojito

At Chef Allen's, July is Mango Madness month. We start by macerating hundreds of pounds of mangoes in gallons of rum so we can put them up for the winter. We never want to let go of those bright, summer flavors. Use ripe Florida mangoes that have the sweet aroma of the tropics for this recipe.

serves **2**

1/2 large Florida mango
6 mint leaves
4 cubes raw sugar
2 tablespoons freshly squeezed lime juice
2 thin slices lime
10 large ice cubes
1/2 cup (4 ounces) mango rum
6 tablespoons (3 ounces) Mountain Dew

Cut the mango into 4 large wedges. Keep 2 of the wedges for garnish. Remove the flesh from the remaining mango and divide between 2 tall glasses. Add the mint leaves, sugar, lime juice and lime slices and muddle the mixture in each glass. Add the ice and mango rum to each glass. Top with a splash of Mountain Dew. Garnish each drink with a reserved mango wedge.

mango rum
3 large ripe Florida mangoes
1 bottle white rum

Peel the mangoes, cut the flesh from the pits and cut into large dice. Put the mangoes in a clean 2-quart mason jar. Add the white rum and seal the jar. Let sit in a cool, dark place for 2 to 3 days before using. Ladle out the mango rum as needed.

mango and crab salad

This salad can be made with most varieties of mango. I prefer the Nam Doc Mai because it has little or no fiber. Very thinly slice the mango flesh to get semicircular slices using a mandoline or sharp knife. Using a three-inch round cookie cutter, cut out twelve circles of mango for the salad. The remaining pieces can be diced for the crab mixture.

serves **4**

3 tablespoons freshly squeezed lime juice
2 tablespoons Thai fish sauce
2 tablespoons sugar
2 medium ripe mangoes, peeled and
    cut from the pit
2 cups fresh lump crab meat, picked over
    for shell
2 tablespoons grated fresh coconut or
    flaked dried coconut
1/2 cup coconut milk
2 tablespoons chopped green onions
1 teaspoon peanut oil
1/8 teaspoon red pepper flakes
10 fresh cilantro leaves
10 fresh basil leaves
10 fresh mint leaves

Combine the lime juice, fish sauce and sugar in a small bowl, stirring to dissolve the sugar. Add the diced mango, crab meat, coconut, coconut milk and green onions to the bowl and mix gently. Cover and refrigerate for 30 minutes.

Add the peanut oil, pepper flakes and herb leaves, tearing them into small pieces as you add them to the bowl. Mix lightly.

Place a 3-inch cookie cutter on a plate and place 1 mango circle in this mold. Fill 3/4 full with the crab mixture. Top with another mango circle and press down lightly to form the crab mango tower while removing the cutter. Repeat with the remaining plates. If you don't have a ring mold, mound the crab meat mixture to layer.

For millions of people around the world, the mango is a comfort food, one of those comestibles that nourishes body and soul. Mangoes are magnificent for cooking. The fruit can absorb spice, heat, and fire with no loss of character. Cooks should use the mango's characteristics to enhance their dishes and strive for a balance of contrasting sweet and tart flavors. Star anise, coriander, clove, vanilla, turmeric, and cardamom all marry well with mango. Spicing the mango can be as simple as a salsa with garlic, cumin, chiles, and cilantro, yet can be icy and refreshing in a sorbet.

handmade mango pastel

I'm astonished at the mango's spectrum of colors: green, pink, red, orange, red-orange, yellow, canary yellow, crimson red, and ruby. And their size can range from the large peach-size Caribbean mango to the Mexican Oro mangoes that are as big as cantaloupes, though slightly flattened.

serves 6

1 1/4 cups all-purpose flour
2 tablespoons sugar
1/4 teaspoon salt
1/2 cup (1 stick) unsalted butter, chilled and
    cut into 1/2-inch pieces
4 ounces cream cheese, chilled and cut into
    1/2-inch pieces
2 teaspoons lime juice

1 tablespoon ice water
2 large ripe mangoes, peeled, pitted and sliced
2 tablespoons lime juice
1/4 cup sugar
1 teaspoon minced ginger
1/4 teaspoon cardamom
2 tablespoons milk
2 tablespoons sugar

Combine the flour, 2 tablespoons sugar and salt in a bowl, using an electric mixer at low speed. Add the butter and cream cheese and mix at medium speed until the mixture is a pebbly consistency. Moisten with 2 teaspoons lime juice and the water, continuing to mix just until the dough forms a ball. Remove from the bowl, cut into 6 pieces and shape into small disks. Transfer to a plate, cover with film and refrigerate for 30 minutes or until firm.

Remove the dough from the refrigerator and let stand for 5 minutes. Roll out the dough into 6-inch circles with a small rolling pin. Place on a baking sheet lined with parchment. Preheat the oven to 400 degrees. Mix together the mangoes, 2 tablespoons lime juice, 1/4 cup sugar, ginger and cardamom in a small bowl. Arrange the mango slices in the center of each pastry shell, leaving a 2-inch edge. Turn this edge up against the mango pieces slightly, enclosing the mango into a tart. Brush the pastry edges with the milk and sprinkle with 2 tablespoons sugar. Bake for 15 minutes or until golden brown and crisp.

Bar none, the mango is the most popular fruit in the world, and every tropical culture uses its native fruit in distinct ways. Cubans love the tiny Toledo mango. In Jamaica, they prize the Julie or East Indian mango. The Edward and the Zill are popular here in South Florida. Even on my travels to the Caribbean, Latin America, and South America, I try to find new varieties; I think I'm up to 200 types. The range of mango flavors is endless. The Manila mango from Mexico has spicy notes of orange and lime zest that give way to flavors of honey, raisin, and hazelnut. The Neelum is an Indian mango with complex aromas of clove and cinnamon with full red-berry, plum, and apricot flavors. The Madame Francis from Haiti has hints of anise, cinnamon, caramel, and fig.

eugenia**theodosopoulos**

Eugenia Theodosopoulos was born in Cambridge, Ohio. At nine years old, she started bussing tables in the family restaurant, which was founded by her grandfather in 1931 and is still operated by her family; it is now called Theo's.

By the age of thirteen, she was baking the already famous pies every day after school with her older sister. After earning a BA in Art History from Syracuse University and working for three years as an event planner in Boston, she decided, at twenty-six, to move to Paris to learn French and attend the famous Ecole Lenôtre, where she also eventually worked. She spent five years in Paris, started a cooking school, and opened a catering company to serve foreign diplomats, embassies, and international executives. Next, she and her new French husband decided to move to Phoenix, Arizona, to start a catering company together.

Essence Catering, now celebrating its tenth anniversary, has built a very loyal clientele by specializing in catering unique parties with premium quality foods. They make all of their petits fours, breads, pastries, and desserts.

Eugenia continues to give cooking classes and is committed to helping underprivileged young kids learn about food. She has created a culinary program to help mentor at-risk kids by giving and organizing cooking classes with different chefs in group homes and homeless shelters. She is also a member of Les Dames d'Escoffier.

Growing up in a restaurant is certainly a unique experience. As an American teenager, I worked seven days a week at the restaurant in addition to school obligations and extracurricular activities. Unlike now, it was not considered a glamorous profession. My friends and my parents' friends certainly never said, "I love to cook; I want to be a chef or have my own restaurant." But they sure did love eating and coming into our restaurant or over to our house for Sunday dinners or special occasions. When we did have any time or day off, we actually cooked more and invited people over to eat.

I have always believed that the best chefs love people and love to make them happy with their food. That is precisely how I got my first date with my husband—I told him I knew how to cook. I am glad that the culinary profession has much more respect these days, but, believe me, it is still just as much work, and I still would never want to do anything else.

Photographer &
Food Stylist
chrisreynolds

The best chefs love people and love to make them happy with their food.

leg of **lamb**

recipesrecipes

Leg of Lamb Simmered in Sweet-and-Sour Pomegranate Sauce

Creamy Yogurt and Cucumber Dip

Luscious Lemon Curd Tart with Toasted Italian Meringue

eugenia**theodosopoulos** 147

leg of lamb simmered in sweet-and-sour pomegranate sauce

I came up with this dish after a dinner in France with our chef friends from Lenôtre, where they served a leg of lamb simmered in a rich broth, and it was delicious. I wanted a more complex flavor to go with the lamb and decided to combine pomegranate molasses, used in many Persian dishes, with cabernet and rosemary. The dish can be perfect for entertaining a small crowd. The entire dish can be prepared ahead of time and reheated at 350 degrees, and, in fact, it tastes even better reheated.

serves **8 to 10**

1 (4- to 5-pound) boned leg of lamb
1 tablespoon olive oil
salt and freshly ground pepper to taste
1 tablespoon olive oil
2 medium onions, chopped into 1-inch pieces
4 large garlic cloves, cut into 4 slices
1 teaspoon toasted ground coriander
1 teaspoon toasted ground cumin
1/4 cup sugar
3 sprigs fresh rosemary
3 sprigs fresh thyme
3/4 bottle cabernet
1/2 cup pomegranate molasses
1/4 cup balsamic vinegar
3 cups rich beef broth or veal broth
1/4 cup (1/2 stick) butter
1/4 cup all-purpose flour
rosemary sprigs and pomegranate seeds,
    for garnish

Preheat the oven to 500 degrees. Rinse the leg of lamb and pat dry. Rub with 1 tablespoon olive oil and season generously with salt and pepper. Place in a large Dutch oven with a lid or a roasting pan with high sides. Sear in the oven for 15 minutes or until golden brown. Remove the lamb from the oven and reduce the oven temperature to 350 degrees.

Heat 1 tablespoon olive oil in a medium saucepan over medium-high heat. Add the onions and sauté for 3 minutes or until wilted. Add the garlic, coriander, cumin, sugar, 3 sprigs rosemary and thyme. Sauté for 2 minutes, stirring constantly. Add the wine, pomegranate molasses, balsamic vinegar and beef broth. Bring to a boil and pour into the Dutch oven with the lamb. Cover tightly with a lid or plastic wrap and foil.

Roast for 2 hours. Turn the lamb over and replace the lid or add new plastic wrap and foil. Roast for 2 1/2 hours longer; the meat should be very tender. Remove the lamb to a platter to cool for 20 minutes. Strain the cooking liquid into a medium saucepan and cook until reduced by 1/3.

Melt the butter in the microwave or a small saucepan and stir in the flour until smooth. Drizzle the mixture slowly into the reduced liquid, whisking constantly. Bring to a boil and cook for 2 minutes, stirring constantly. Taste and adjust the seasonings.

Slice the lamb 1/2 inch thick and fan out in a serving dish or baking dish. Cover the lamb slices with the sauce. Serve immediately or chill for up to 2 days and reheat to serve. Garnish with additional rosemary sprigs and pomegranate seeds. Serve with steamed rice or—my favorite—over thick slices of country bread with wilted baby spinach.

creamy yogurt and cucumber dip

makes **3¹/2 cups**

1 seedless cucumber
1 teaspoon salt
32 ounces plain whole milk yogurt
2/3 cup sour cream
1 teaspoon sugar
2 tablespoons red wine vinegar
1 large garlic clove, pressed in a garlic press
3 tablespoons extra-virgin olive oil
salt and freshly ground pepper to taste
chopped chives or dill, for garnish

Peel the cucumber and cut into halves lengthwise. Remove any seeds with a spoon and discard. Grate in a food processor or by hand and toss in a bowl with 1 teaspoon salt. Place in a colander to drain with a weight on top. Let stand in the refrigerator for 4 hours or at room temperature for 1 hour. Place the yogurt in a colander lined with paper towels and let stand in the refrigerator for 4 hours or at room temperature for 1 hour.

Remove the cucumber and yogurt from the colanders and combine in a mixing bowl. Add the sour cream, sugar, red wine vinegar, garlic and olive oil and stir to mix well. Season with salt and pepper to taste. Refrigerate for about 2 hours before serving. Garnish with chopped chives or dill and serve with pita bread, fresh-cut vegetables and olives.

My dad used to make his own yogurt, and it was so good we would put it on everything. My favorite way to eat it was with steaming hot rice pilaf. I still love yogurt and made this version of tzatziki that my mom, dad, and whole family love. It's delicious with everything from roasted chicken, grilled fish, and fresh beets to the more typical flatbreads and vegetable crudités. It is one of our most requested spreads.

luscious lemon curd tart
with toasted italian meringue

This recipe is dedicated to my good friend and mentor Jean-Louis Clement, MOF, 1997. Don't be daunted by the three steps or the cooked sugar in the Italian meringue. All three components are delicious and can be used in many different ways. I guarantee, it will all be worth it in the end. The sablé pastry makes enough for two tarts and can also be rolled out for cookies. The curd filling is also delicious with scones and biscuits or served in a decorative glass cup layered with blueberries and Greek-style yogurt and topped with a sablé cookie and almond slivers.

makes **two 8-inch tarts**

7 ounces European-style butter, cut into
    small pieces
grated zest of 3 lemons
6 large eggs

1 1/2 cups sugar
3/4 cup lemon juice, from the 3 zested lemons
1 sablé pastry
Italian meringue

Combine the butter and lemon zest in a saucepan over medium heat. Bring to a gentle boil, swirling to combine. Boil for 2 minutes to eliminate the solids from the butter. Whisk the eggs and sugar together in a mixing bowl. Add the lemon juice and drizzle in the boiling butter gradually, whisking constantly. Return to the saucepan over medium-high heat. Bring to a boil, stirring constantly with a heatproof spatula or wooden spoon. Reduce the heat to medium and cook, stirring, for 2 minutes longer. Strain into a glass or stainless steel bowl, pressing the solids to remove the liquid. Place a film directly on the surface and chill for up to 2 days.

Spoon the lemon mixture into the baked sablé crust and smooth with a spatula. Decorate with the meringue in 1 of 3 ways: spoon the meringue into a pastry bag fitted with a large star tip and pipe large star-shaped swirls on the top; place a pastry ring the size of the tart on the top and fill with the meringue, smoothing with a palette knife; or dollop large spoonfuls of the meringue over the top, starting at the outer edge and making circles toward the center.

Brown the meringue with a torch or bake in a preheated 400-degree oven for 4 minutes or until lightly toasted. Cut into wedges to serve with a mixture of berries.

sablé pastry

5 ounces European-style butter, at room
    temperature
$^1/_3$ cup plus 2 tablespoons confectioners'
    sugar, sifted
2 tablespoons finely ground blanched almonds
$^1/_2$ teaspoon salt
$^3/_4$ teaspoon vanilla extract
1 egg
$1^3/_4$ cups all-purpose flour

Place the butter in the bowl of a mixer fitted with a paddle attachment and cream until smooth. Add the confectioners' sugar, ground almonds, salt and vanilla and mix well. Add the egg and half the flour. Add the remaining flour and mix until the dough comes away from the side of the bowl and forms a loose mass. Turn out onto a board and gently press together. Cut into 2 balls; chill 1 ball for 2 hours to overnight and freeze the second for another use.

Let the chilled dough stand at room temperature for 10 minutes. Roll $^1/_4$ inch thick on a lightly floured surface and place in a straight-sided 8-inch tart shell or 9-inch pie plate. Do not worry if it breaks; simply press it back together to appear seamless. Pierce with a fork all over and place in the refrigerator for 15 minutes to rest.

Bake at 350 degrees on the middle oven rack for 12 minutes or until golden brown.

italian meringue

$^3/_4$ cup sugar
$^1/_2$ cup water
4 large egg whites
$^1/_2$ teaspoon cream of tartar, or squeeze
    of lemon juice
2 tablespoons sugar

Combine $^3/_4$ cup sugar and $^1/_4$ cup of the water in a small heavy-bottomed saucepan. Cook, whisking, over medium-high heat just until the sugar dissolves. Continue to cook without stirring. Place the remaining $^1/_4$ cup water in a small glass cup and use a pastry brush to brush the sugar crystals down from the side of the saucepan; be sure that the brush is clean of grease, butter, etc., or the meringue will deflate. Place a candy thermometer in the sugar mixture.

Combine the egg whites with the cream of tartar in a mixing bowl and mix at medium speed for 4 minutes. Wipe down the side of the

saucepan with the sugar mixture 2 more times while the egg whites are mixing. Increase the speed of the mixer to medium-high and beat until almost firm. Add 2 tablespoons sugar and beat until firm but not dry.

Cook the sugar mixture to 248 to 250 degrees on the candy thermometer, firm-ball stage. Pour the mixture slowly into the egg whites by the side of the bowl rather than on the beater attachment, beating constantly at high speed. Beat for 2 minutes and reduce the speed to medium-low to cool, about 20 minutes. You can prepare this up to 8 hours in advance and store in the freezer.

terry**thompson-anderson**

Terry Thompson-Anderson is a seasoned culinary professional. She has written three cookbooks, *Cajun-Creole Cooking, Eating Southern Style,* and the critically acclaimed *Texas on the Plate.*

Her first book, *Cajun-Creole Cooking*, first published in 1986, is now in its third revision, and there are half a million copies in print. She is currently working on a new book entitled *Lone Star Eats*.

Terry is a passionate cook, constantly creating new flavor combinations to share with fellow food lovers. She has written for numerous national and local publications, spreading her gospel of good flavors. She is a popular speaker at culinary symposia and a highly regarded cooking teacher, having taught more than 20,000 students in her career. Terry has made numerous media appearances, including a live presentation during the *Fox and Friends* segment in Times Square in New York City.

At one time, Terry was the chef/owner of Café Raintree in Bay St. Louis, Mississippi, and later served as executive chef for the Halliburton Corporation's three executive lodges in the Texas coastal marshlands, where she fed dignitaries from around the world for twelve years. She recently relocated to Fredericksburg, in the heart of central Texas Hill Country, with her husband, Roger, to work as the director of culinary development for Fischer and Wieser specialty foods. Terry is a charter member of IACP and has attained the IACP's CCP designation. She is also a member of Les Dames d'Escoffier International.

Photographer
toddtrice

Food Stylist
danmacey

Create harmony among the ingredients and make them do a little tango in your mouth.

avocado **cream soup**

t t

recipesrecipes

Avocado Cream Soup with Lime and Chile Tortilla Strips

Grilled Duck Breast with Roasted Poblano Chile and Garlic Sauce

Braised Beef Short Ribs in Ancho Chile Gravy with Morels

Curry-Fried Oysters with Texas Peach Rémoulade Sauce and Pico de Gallo

terry**thompson-anderson** 153

avocado cream soup
with lime and chile tortilla strips

This great chilled soup tastes like the very essence of summer in Texas. It's sultry and spicy, smooth with crispy highlights, and it will make you feel good—just like summer in Texas. I first developed this recipe for a winery luncheon at Spicewood Vineyard as part of the 2003 Texas Hill Country Food and Wine Festival. It has since been featured in the *Houston Chronicle* and *Texas Journeys Magazine.*

serves **8 to 10**

4 ripe Haas avocados, cut into 1-inch pieces
1/2 cup packed cilantro leaves and tender
   top stems
3 serrano chiles, seeds and veins removed,
   coarsely chopped
1 quart good-quality chicken stock
1 cup whipping cream
1/4 cup freshly squeezed lime juice
salt to taste
sour cream
lime and chile tortilla strips
chopped cilantro, for garnish
pico de gallo (page 157)

lime and chile tortilla strips
10 white corn tortillas
canola oil for deep-frying
4 pasilla chiles, or 2 tablespoons
   good-quality chili powder
lime-flavored beer salt

Combine the avocados, 1/2 cup cilantro, chiles and 1 1/2 cups of the chicken stock in a blender and process until very smooth. Transfer to a medium bowl and whisk in the remaining chicken stock, whipping cream, lime juice and salt. Taste for seasoning and adjust the salt if the soup tastes flat and boring. Cover and chill well before serving.

Ladle the soup into soup plates and top with a dollop of sour cream. Nest a bunch of lime and chile tortilla strips on the sour cream and scatter some of the chopped cilantro and pico de gallo over the tortilla strips.

Cut the tortilla strips into halves and then into strips 1/4 inch wide. Deep-fry in canola oil preheated to 350 degrees until crisp and very light brown, about 2 to 3 minutes. Drain on wire racks.

Remove the seeds from the pasilla chiles and toast them in a dry cast-iron skillet over medium-high heat until very crisp; do not burn. Grind the chiles to a powder in a spice mill or coffee grinder. Toss the ground chiles with some of the lime salt in a small bowl and season the tortilla strips liberally with the mixture; the strips should be dark in color from the chiles. Store in an airtight container.

There is an art to seasoning foods that will be served cold, such as this soup. Cold dulls the senses of hot, sweet, salty, and spicy on our tongues. Therefore, you should slightly over-season foods that will be served cold, or they will taste very bland once they have been refrigerated, and then it is hard to adjust the seasonings. So don't be stingy with the salt in this soup, or it just won't reach its full flavor potential.

grilled duck breast
with roasted poblano chile and garlic sauce

Properly grilled duck breast is one of the most delicious meats I know. There is such a deep, rich flavor comprised of the taste of the grill, the tenderness from the wonderful fatty skin, and the slightly musky flavor of the meat itself. Add a really wonderful sauce, and your taste buds are in heaven!

serves **4**

4 (8-ounce) duck breasts with skin
extra-virgin olive oil
salt and freshly ground black pepper
roasted poblano chile and garlic sauce

Heat a gas grill to medium-high. Baste the duck breasts liberally with olive oil and season both sides with salt and pepper. Place skin side down on the grill rack and grill for about 7 minutes, basting frequently with olive oil. Turn the duck and grill for an additional 3 minutes.

Cut the duck into thin slices on the bias. Fan the slices out on individual serving plates and spoon the roasted poblano chile and garlic sauce over each serving.

roasted poblano chile and garlic sauce

1/4 cup peanut oil
1 small onion, chopped
2 large Roma tomatoes, blistered, peeled
    and chopped
4 poblano chiles, roasted, peeled, seeded
    and chopped
6 large garlic cloves, roasted
1 teaspoon dried Mexican oregano
1 quart chicken stock
salt to taste
1 medium red bell pepper, blistered, peeled,
    seeded and finely chopped
1/4 cup minced fresh cilantro

Heat the peanut oil in a heavy 3-quart saucepan over medium-high heat. Add the onion and sauté until light brown and very wilted, about 15 minutes, stirring frequently. Add the tomatoes, chiles, garlic and oregano. Sauté, stirring frequently, for about 20 minutes or until the vegetables are very pulpy. Add the chicken stock and cook until the liquid is reduced by half, about 25 to 30 minutes.

Purée the sauce in batches in a blender or food processor fitted with a steel blade. Combine the batches in the saucepan and season with salt. Stir in the red bell pepper and cilantro. Cook for 5 minutes. Serve hot.

braised beef short ribs
in ancho chile gravy with morels

4 ancho chiles

8 pounds beef short ribs

salt and freshly ground black
pepper to taste

1/2 cup plus 3 tablespoons
extra-virgin olive oil

2 ribs celery, chopped

3 large carrots, peeled and
chopped

1 large onion, chopped

1/2 cup tomato paste

5 sprigs fresh thyme

3 fresh bay leaves

1 tablespoon whole black
peppercorns

3 anchovy fillets, minced

20 garlic cloves, smashed with
the blade of a chef's knife

2 cups cabernet sauvignon

1/3 cup red wine vinegar

4 cups beef stock

2 ounces dried morels

3 heaping tablespoons red
currant jelly

2 tablespoons cornstarch

1/2 cup beef stock

cooked egg noodles

minced parsley, for garnish

Beef short ribs are an underutilized, yet delicious, cut of meat. The main drawback to serving them in today's hurried world is that they take a long time to cook to be at their tender best. This dish, however, is well worth the time involved in ratio to the magnificent rich taste of the finished dish. I like to call it one of those upscale-down-home dishes! In finalizing the sauce for the dish, I use one of my favorite chef's secrets to add just the right touch of balance—red currant jelly.

Cover the ancho chiles with hot water in a bowl and let stand until soft and pliable. Season the short ribs liberally with salt and pepper. Heat 1/2 cup olive oil in a heavy 12-inch skillet over medium-high heat. Add the ribs and sear, turning frequently to brown evenly to a hazelnut color on all sides. Transfer to a roasting pan large enough to hold them in a single layer; discard the olive oil in the skillet.

Drain and mince the chiles, discarding the stems and seeds. Heat 3 tablespoons olive oil in a heavy 5-quart saucepan over medium-high heat. Add the celery, carrots, onion and chiles and sauté, stirring frequently, until the onion is wilted and transparent, about 8 minutes. Stir in the tomato paste. Cook, stirring constantly, for about 2 to 3 minutes or until the tomato paste is slightly brown. Stir in the thyme, bay leaves, peppercorns, anchovies and garlic. Cook for 10 minutes.

Preheat the oven to 325 degrees. Stir the wine and vinegar into the sauce and bring to a boil over high heat. Add 4 cups beef stock, reduce the heat, and simmer for 10 minutes.

Pour over the ribs in the roasting pan. Cover the pan and roast for 1 hour. Remove the cover and roast for 3 hours longer or until very tender.

Cover the morels with hot water in a mixing bowl 30 minutes before the ribs are done and let stand until soft and pliable. Remove the ribs to a serving platter and strain the liquid in the pan, pressing down on the vegetables to extract all of the flavorful broth.

Skim the fat from the broth and transfer the broth to a heavy 4-quart saucepan. Drain the morels, discarding the water. Add the morels and jelly to the saucepan and bring to a full rolling boil. Whisk in a mixture of the cornstarch and 1/2 cup beef stock. Cook just until the mixture thickens, stirring constantly.

Spoon egg noodles onto each serving plate. Nest 3 or 4 ribs in the noodles and spoon a generous portion of the sauce over the top. Garnish with minced parsley and serve hot.

curry-fried oysters with texas peach rémoulade sauce and pico de gallo

I love oysters just about any way you can prepare them—or not prepare them. I love them raw on the half shell most of all. This dish is just for all of the other oyster lovers out there. The sauce has a nice kick to it—what I like to call a "fiesta for your mouth"—that pairs beautifully with the hint of curry in the oyster batter. The secret to the success of the dish is that the oysters must be cooked just until the moment a crust forms, then drained. They should have that nice paper-thin crust from the batter, but still be almost liquid inside.

serves **4 to 6**

4 cups Louisiana Fish Fry seasoning
1¹/2 teaspoons salt
1¹/2 teaspoons finely ground black pepper
1 teaspoon granulated garlic
2 tablespoons curry powder
36 medium oysters, shucked
6 eggs
6 cups milk
canola oil for deep-frying
texas peach rémoulade sauce
pico de gallo

Season the Louisiana Fish Fry with the salt, pepper, garlic and curry powder in a bowl. Pat the oysters very dry with absorbent paper towels. Dip each oyster into a mixture of the eggs and milk, coating well. Press in the curry-seasoned Fish Fry, coating well and shaking off the excess.

Heat canola oil to 350 degrees in a deep fryer. Deep-fry the oysters in small batches in the oil, taking care not to crowd them in the oil and frying just until a golden crust forms. Remove to wire racks to drain. Serve hot with the Texas peach rémoulade sauce and pico de gallo for dipping.

pico de gallo

5 Roma tomatoes, finely diced into
   ¹/4-inch pieces
2 serrano chiles, seeds and veins removed,
   minced
¹/4 cup finely chopped onion
2 tablespoons chopped cilantro
2 teaspoons lime juice
salt to taste

Combine all the ingredients in a bowl and chill until ready to use. Do not add the salt until serving time if you are making the pico more than 2 hours in advance, as it will make the tomatoes weep and water down the pico.

texas peach rémoulade sauce

2 cups mayonnaise
¹/4 cup whole-grain mustard, such as
   Moutarde de Meaux
3 green onions with green tops, minced
1¹/2 tablespoons minced flat-leaf Italian parsley
1 chipotle chile in adobo sauce, minced
1 tablespoon freshly squeezed lemon juice
1 tablespoon Worcestershire sauce
12 large garlic cloves, minced
¹/2 teaspoon salt, or to taste
¹/2 teaspoon cayenne pepper
pinch of finely ground black pepper
7 tablespoons Texas peach preserves

Combine the mayonnaise, mustard, green onions, parsley, chipotle chile, lemon juice, Worcestershire sauce, garlic, salt, cayenne pepper, black pepper and preserves in a food processor fitted with a steel blade; process until smooth. Store in a container with a tight-fitting lid in the refrigerator. Serve at room temperature.

charlie**trotter**

Charlie Trotter started cooking professionally in 1982 after graduating from the University of Wisconsin. At that time, he embarked on an intense four-year period of work, study, and travel. He lived in Chicago, San Francisco, Florida, and Europe, "reading every cookbook I could get my hands on, working like a maniac, and eating out incessantly."

Harvey Steinman from the *Wine Spectator* observes that "Trotter regards recipes the way jazz musicians see their musical scores as frameworks for improvisation. The results follow a discipline, but they spring from the moment, not a carefully plotted script." His adept understanding of cultural influences and flavors from around the world are intuitively and spontaneously translated into his own highly original cuisine—cuisine that is simply unparalleled.

Charlie Trotter's is regarded as one of the finest restaurants in the world. For over seventeen years, the restaurant has dedicated itself to excellence in the culinary arts. The restaurant is recognized by a variety of prestigious national and international institutions. In 1995, Charlie Trotter's was inducted into the esteemed Relais & Chateaux and in 1998 was accepted as a member by Traditions & Qualité. It is the only Chicago restaurant to receive five stars from the *Mobil Travel Guide*, has a five diamonds designation from AAA, and has seven James Beard Foundation awards, including Outstanding Restaurant (2000) and Outstanding Chef (1999). *Wine Spectator* named the restaurant The Best Restaurant in the World for Wine & Food (1998) and America's Best Restaurant (2000).

Chef Trotter is the author of nine cookbooks and is the host of the nationally aired, award-winning PBS cooking series, *The Kitchen Sessions with Charlie Trotter*. Beyond his numerous culinary accolades, Chef Trotter is very involved in a large number of national and international philanthropic activities, including the Charlie Trotter Culinary Education Foundation. Since 1999, Chef Trotter has hosted biweekly dinners for high school students and underwritten annual fund-raising dinners for the foundation, raising over $400,000 for individuals seeking careers in the culinary arts. Chef Trotter recently received an award at the White House from President Bush and Colin Powell for his work with the foundation and was named one of only five Heroes to be honored by Colin Powell's charity, America's Promise.

Photographer & Food Stylist
kiplingswehla

...has been instrumental in establishing new standards for fine dining worldwide

lobster with hokkaido squash soup and brown butter

recipesrecipes

Lobster with Hokkaido Squash Soup and Brown Butter

Serrano Ham and Phyllo-Wrapped Salsify with Bosc Pear and Caramelized Endive

Bison with Root Vegetable Pavé and Parsnip Purée

charlietrotter 159

lobster with hokkaido squash soup and brown butter

1 Hokkaido squash, cut into
   halves and seeds removed
1 tablespoon extra-virgin
   olive oil
1 teaspoon ground star anise
salt and freshly ground black
   pepper to taste
3 cups water
1 cup freshly squeezed
   orange juice
1 tablespoon rice wine vinegar
1 tablespoon butter
24 stems watercress, thick
   stems trimmed away
reserved lobster juices
1 cup finely chopped
   water chestnuts
2 tablespoons finely chopped
   Granny Smith apple
lobster
1 orange, peeled, sectioned
   and sections cut into thirds
brown butter
1 tablespoon finely grated
   orange zest
1/4 teaspoon ground star anise

Lobster and squash are already a superb combination, but this interpretation, with its textural and flavorful notes of citrus, apple, and watercress, reaches a higher level. Peppery watercress provides a magnificent contrast, cutting through the sweeter components. Star anise is lightly dusted over the lobster meat and soup for just the right hint of exoticism.

Preheat the oven to 375 degrees. Rub the inside of the squash with the olive oil and 1 teaspoon star anise; season with salt and pepper. Place cut side down in an ovenproof pan and add 1 cup of the water. Roast the squash for 1½ hours, or until tender. Remove the pulp from the skin and purée the pulp in a blender with the remaining 2 cups water, orange juice, and vinegar until smooth. If the soup is too thick, add additional orange juice and water. Transfer the soup to a saucepan and warm over medium heat; whisk in the butter and season with salt and pepper. Keep warm over low heat.

Toss the watercress in the reserved lobster juices in a bowl; season with salt and pepper. Reserve 8 stems for garnish. Arrange some of the water chestnuts, the apple, and remaining watercress in the centers of 4 shallow serving bowls. Divide the lobster among the 4 bowls and arrange in an overlapping row atop the watercress. Sprinkle the orange sections around the bowl. Carefully pour some of the soup into each bowl around the lobster. Drizzle some of the brown butter over the lobster and around the soup. Sprinkle the orange zest and ¼ teaspoon star anise over the soup and lobster and arrange the reserved watercress over the lobster.

lobster and brown butter
3/4 cup (1½ sticks) butter
4 small lobster tails, cooked and cut into
   1/3-inch-thick medallions
salt and freshly ground black pepper

Place the butter in a small saucepan and melt over medium-low heat. Continue to simmer slowly, allowing the milk solids to rise to the top. Skim off the milk solids. Cook until the butter has a nutty aroma and there are dark brown specks in the bottom of the pan.

Preheat the oven to 400 degrees. Arrange the lobster medallions flat in an ovenproof pan; drizzle with 1½ tablespoons of the brown butter and season with salt and pepper. Bake for 2 minutes, or just until hot. Remove the lobster from the pan and reserve the juices in the pan.

Wine note: the hokkaido squash soup is rich with a low level of acidity and is accented by an apple and orange garnish. The full-bodied Cuvée Sainte Catherine Riesling from Domaine Weinbach has lively acidity that cuts through the brown butter and reveals the citrus notes. A Pinot Blanc from Chalone accentuates the spice notes and makes another stellar pairing.

serrano ham and phyllo-wrapped salsify
with bosc pear and caramelized endive

In this simple but sophisticated recipe, crispy phyllo encases spears of sweet poached salsify wrapped in slices of richly satisfying serrano ham. Pieces of the phyllo rolls, along with braised Belgian endive, are then placed on a smear of satiny salsify purée to accentuate that extraordinary flavor. Slices of sautéed pear provide the perfect sweetness to contrast the bitter flavor of the endive and to cut into the rich and salty taste of the ham. A drizzle of the vinaigrette provides the final emphasis on the bitter and sweet accents.

Combine the milk and lemon juice in a saucepan large enough that the salsify can lie flat. Peel the salsify and trim the ends. Place the salsify in the saucepan, add water to cover and the bay leaves, peppercorns and thyme. Bring to a slow simmer and cook until al dente. Remove the salsify from the liquid, reserving the liquid. Coarsely chop 2 of the salsify stalks; pick 2 that do not match the others in size. Process the chopped salsify with just enough of the reserved cooking liquid in a blender until smooth. Just prior to serving, season the purée with salt and pepper and reheat.

Preheat the oven to 375 degrees and line a sheet pan with baking parchment. Lay 1 sheet of the phyllo on a flat work surface and lightly brush with some of the melted butter and sprinkle with some of the basil. Carefully lay 2 more sheets of the phyllo atop the first, brushing each sheet with some of the butter and sprinkling with some of the basil; trim the edges. Repeat the process with the remaining phyllo. Top each phyllo stack with some of the ham and arrange 2 stalks of the salsify side by side over the ham. Roll up the stacks like a cigar, secure with a light coating of the butter and brush the outside layer of the rolls with the remaining butter. Arrange the phyllo wraps in a single layer on the prepared sheet pan and bake for 20 minutes or until golden brown and crispy. Trim the ends of the rolls and slice each diagonally into 4 portions.

Melt 2 tablespoons butter in a sauté pan over medium-high heat and add the endive cut side down. Cook for 5 minutes on each side or until caramelized. Add the sugar and water and cover. Continue to cook for 10 minutes longer or until the endive is tender. Remove the endive and season with salt and pepper.

Spoon some of the salsify purée down the center of each plate. Place 2 endive quarters in the center of each plate and lay a few pear slices around the endive. Place 2 pieces of the phyllo-wrapped salsify atop the pears and drizzle the vinaigrette around the plate. Sprinkle with the parsley and pepper.

sautéed pear
1 Bosc pear, cut into $1/8$-inch slices
1 tablespoon butter
salt and freshly ground black pepper to taste

Sauté the pear in the butter in a sauté pan over medium heat for 6 minutes or until golden brown. Season with salt and pepper.

vinaigrette
1 shallot, minced
$1/4$ cup finely chopped Asian pear
2 tablespoons apple cider vinegar
6 tablespoons extra-virgin olive oil
$1/2$ cup finely chopped red Belgian endive
1 tablespoon chopped fresh chives
salt and freshly ground black pepper to taste

Combine the shallot, pear and vinegar in a small bowl. Add the olive oil gradually, whisking constantly. Stir in the endive and chives and season with salt and pepper.

Wine note: The richness of this full-flavored dish is cut slightly and lightened by the bitterness of the endive, the saltiness of the ham, and the bright acid of a Jackson Estate Sauvignon Blanc. The passion fruit and grapefruit notes of this Marlborough Sauvignon Blanc are brightened by the dish and complement the pears.

2 cups milk
juice of $1/2$ lemon
6 stalks salsify
2 bay leaves
1 teaspoon peppercorns
3 sprigs of thyme
salt and freshly ground black pepper to taste
6 sheets phyllo pastry
$1/2$ cup (1 stick) butter, melted
$1/4$ cup chopped fresh basil
4 ounces serrano ham, thinly sliced
2 tablespoons butter
2 heads red Belgian endive, cut into quarters
1 tablespoon sugar
$1/2$ cup water
sautéed pear
vinaigrette
$1/4$ cup micro parsley or chopped fresh parsley

bison with root vegetable pavé and parsnip purée

Although this preparation is relatively straightforward, the result is both elegant and soul-satisfying. A bite of the pavé melts in the mouth with the distinctive and subtle flavors of the root vegetables, and the bison tenderloin is a special treat indeed (though beef or chicken, or even tuna or lobster, can easily be substituted). A pool of very loose parsnip purée brings a glorious creaminess to the plate, and a small drizzle of intense meat jus is all that is required to complete this very regal dish.

serves 4

2 tablespoons butter, melted
1 celery root, peeled and thinly sliced
4 carrots, peeled and thinly sliced
1 rutabaga, peeled and thinly sliced
4 parsnips, peeled and thinly sliced
1 sweet potato, peeled and thinly sliced
5 cups heavy cream

salt and freshly ground black pepper to taste
parsnip purée
bison tenderloin
1 cup hot meat stock reduction
2 teaspoons fresh rosemary leaves
4 teaspoons extra-virgin olive oil

Preheat the oven to 350 degrees. Line an 8×8-inch pan with foil and brush the foil with 1½ teaspoons of the butter. Place the vegetable slices in 5 separate bowls. Add 1 cup of the heavy cream to each bowl and toss gently to coat evenly.

Arrange a layer of the celery root slices overlapping slightly in the prepared pan and lightly season with salt and pepper. Continue to layer with the carrots, rutabaga, parsnips and sweet potato overlapping slightly until all the vegetables are used and seasoning each layer lightly with salt and pepper. Cover the pan tightly with a second sheet of foil brushed with 1½ teaspoons of the butter. Place another 8×8-inch pan over the foil and weight it down with a brick or other heavy ovenproof object. Bake for 2½ hours or until the vegetables are tender. Chill for 4 to 24 hours, leaving the weight on the pan.

Remove the weight, top pan and foil from the pavé and invert onto a sheet pan. Discard the foil and cut four 2-inch squares from the pavé. Store the remaining pavé in the refrigerator for several days.

Heat the remaining 1 tablespoon butter in a large nonstick sauté pan over medium-high heat. Add the pavé squares and cook for 3 to 4 minutes or until golden brown. Turn and cook for 3 to 4 minutes longer or until heated through. If the pavé is not warm in the middle, heat in a 375-degree oven for 5 minutes.

Spoon some of the parsnip purée in the center of each of 4 dinner plates. Arrange 1 piece of the pavé just left of the center on each plate and arrange the sliced bison in the center. Spoon the stock reduction over the bison and around the plates. Sprinkle evenly with the rosemary leaves and drizzle with the olive oil.

Wine note: Cabernet Franc-based wines, such as Saumur-Champigny from the Loire Valley or Sirita from the Napa Valley, succeed in stressing the earthy notes of the pavé. The full-bodied Sirita rounds out the dish, while the Cabernet Franc from the Loire has a higher level of acidity that cleanses the palate. Château de Villeneuve and Clos Rougeard both produce great examples of Saumur-Champigny.

parsnip purée

¹/₂ cup chopped peeled parsnip
¹/₂ cup milk
salt and freshly ground black pepper to taste

Combine the parsnip and milk in a saucepan and cook over medium-low heat for 10 minutes or until the parsnip is tender. Process the parsnip with enough of the milk in a food processor until puréed. Season with salt and pepper.

bison tenderloin

1 tablespoon grapeseed oil
4 (6-ounce) bison tenderloin pieces
salt and freshly ground black pepper to taste

Preheat the grill to medium. Brush the grapeseed oil over the bison and season with salt and pepper. Grill the bison for 5 to 7 minutes per side or until medium-rare. Remove the bison from the grill and let rest for 3 minutes. Trim the ends and cut each slice into 3 pieces. Season with salt and pepper.

julia**usher**

Though formally trained at the Cambridge School of Culinary Arts, Julia Usher's make-it-yourself approach and eclectic cake-decorating style came from her mother, a self-taught baker, herb gardener, and collector extraordinaire.

In 1995, while still in culinary school and planning her own wedding, Usher was disturbed by the plethora of bland white cakes and unimaginative cake designs on the market. She knew that by combining intense flavor and high style, a well-designed dessert could cast a magical mood. Barely down the aisle, she opened AzucArte, a boutique bakery specializing in such sweets.

After seven years, Julia has custom-made thousands of desserts for society weddings and other special events. Her attention to what's in, on, and around her sweets has put her at the forefront of dessert design. Usher's desserts and cakes have appeared on the cover of *Chocolatier* and in the pages of *Vera Wang on Weddings, Party Art and Design,* and many other national bridal magazines. Usher co-authored an article on holiday cakes that appeared in Mary Engelbreit's *Home Companion,* and her desserts have also been featured at the James Beard House in New York City. She is a former president of the St. Louis Culinary Society.

My first recollections of my mom's obsession for fresh foods date back to third grade, when she and my dad moved with me and my two siblings to an old farmhouse in Guilford, Connecticut, built in 1798. My mom loved old things and history, perhaps as much as food, and was a stickler for authenticity. So naturally, she wanted our "new" old house on Long Hill Road to be just as it was in the eighteenth century! She quickly busied herself with re-creating the southside herb garden, filling it with herbs we rarely hear of today, and rebuilding and restocking the rundown chicken coop with a flock of Rhode Island Reds. She also put dad to work in the neglected blackberry brambles on the perimeter of the ten-acre property, and, in fairly short order, he had tamed them into a prosperous and regular summer crop. My siblings and I watched in wonder, not having any inkling as to how this commotion would ultimately affect our eating habits. The upshot of it all was that, while other Guilford kids munched on peanut butter and grape jelly sandwiches on white bread, we had imaginative lunchbox alternatives like chicken salad laden with lovage and local orchard apples; homemade anadama bread smothered in apple-rose geranium jelly; and blackberry-rhubarb crumble doused with orange mint-infused cream.

apple-rose **geranium** sorbet

Photographer
rickmeoli

Food Stylist
marysutkus

...never eaten a store-bought cake and always orders dessert before the main course

recipesrecipes

Apple-Rose Geranium Sorbet

Scallop, Fennel and Orange Risotto

apple-rose geranium sorbet

There's no flavor from my youth more memorable than the apple-rose geranium pairing that my mom used in her famous jelly. She hasn't made that recipe in years, but I think my frozen derivative captures its uncommonly delicate, yet at the same time powerful, essence. Rose geranium is not usually found in supermarkets, but it's readily available at most garden centers and on the Internet at sites like linglesherbs.com. It's easily cultivated, too. I haven't the slightest green thumb, but my geraniums are thriving, even in the hot and humid Missouri climate where I live.

makes 1³/4 cups before churning

1¹/2 cups unsweetened apple juice
³/4 cup sugar
10 fresh rose geranium leaves, torn, with stems
    discarded (less than¹/2 ounce)
3 tablespoons freshly squeezed lemon juice

Combine the apple juice, sugar and rose geranium leaves in a stainless steel saucepan. Bring to a simmer and remove from the heat.

Let steep for 10 to 15 minutes; strain. Combine the mixture with the lemon juice in a bowl and chill for several hours.

Churn the mixture until creamy and thick in an ice cream maker, using the manufacturer's instructions. If the sorbet is still loose after churning, place it in a sealed container and freeze for 2 to 3 hours or until of scooping consistency.

As tasty as my mother's cooking may sound, my early food experiences weren't all fun, innovation, and sensory pleasure. Like any young kid, I was at first suspicious of the plethora of green things served. I'd ruthlessly cull leaves from my mom's prized recipes and reject them, limp and lifeless, plate-side, as my mom watched in dismay. And, as if my suspicions weren't enough, I was sometimes downright resentful. Why couldn't I eat just like any other normal kid? Why should I have to bundle up from head to toe to change the hens' water in sub-zero temperature, or brave the briers in mid-August, when eggs and blackberries were packaged and poised for the taking in every grocery store? And why was I expected to harvest tarragon or sweet woodruff or whatever mom needed more of in the kitchen, when I knew we could find conveniently dried and bottled substitutes?

You see, my mom would have it no other way. She didn't just love food; she loved the very process of it. From growing to collecting to sharing, these steps were all an equally valuable part of the whole experience. Without this process, food was just something to put in our mouths; but, with it, food became an extension of her, an offering of her heart and soul to those she loved most, and a way to bring her family closer together. It's this lesson of love that I honor here with some of my mom's favorite recipes and others that I've created or adapted to include her favorite green things.

scallop, fennel and orange risotto

I was first turned on to risotto during my CSCA years, after a lecture from a visiting chef-turned-author, Rosario del Nero. I was entranced by his delightfully illustrated book, but more so by the ease with which he transformed arborio rice into a diverse array of dishes by overlaying ever-so-slight twists on the basic foundation. I was amazed that something so tasty could be so simple.

Since my day-to-day work as a pastry chef is incredibly exacting, especially when I'm fussing with wedding cakes, I try not to complicate my cooking during off-hours. I love one-pot meals like this one that are straightforward and incorporate so many of my favorite flavors.

serves **12**

6 tablespoons (³/4 stick) unsalted butter
¹/2 cup finely chopped yellow onion
³/4 cup finely chopped fresh fennel
2 cups uncooked arborio rice, about 1 pound
2 tablespoons fennel seeds
1¹/2 cups freshly squeezed orange juice
1¹/2 cups dry white wine
5 cups fish stock or bottled clam juice,
    or as needed
1¹/2 pounds fresh scallops
1 tablespoon minced orange zest
3 tablespoons freshly grated Parmesan cheese
salt and freshly ground black pepper to taste
chiffonade of fresh basil and grated Parmesan
    cheese, for garnish

Melt the butter in a large stockpot over medium-low heat. Add the onion and fennel and sauté until tender and translucent, about 5 to 10 minutes. Add the rice and fennel seeds. Sauté, stirring constantly, until the rice is translucent around the edges and the fennel seeds are lightly toasted, about 2 to 3 minutes; stir with a wooden spoon, as it is unlikely to break the rice kernels and cause them to absorb the liquid too quickly.

Increase the heat to medium and add the orange juice. Cook until the juice is absorbed, stirring regularly to prevent the rice from sticking. Add the wine and cook until it is absorbed. Add the fish stock 1 cup at a time and cook until the liquid is absorbed after each addition, stirring regularly; the cooking process will take 35 to 40 minutes and may require more or less fish stock, depending on the cooking speed and rice.

Cut extra-large scallops into smaller pieces to ensure even cooking. Add the scallops to the rice in the last 5 to 10 minutes of cooking time. Reduce the heat to low and cook until the scallops are just cooked through and the rice is al dente. Remove from the heat and stir in the orange zest and 3 tablespoons Parmesan cheese. Taste for saltiness, since the fish stock or clam juice can vary considerably in salt content, before seasoning with salt and pepper. Garnish with the chiffonade of basil and additional Parmesan cheese.

food **photographer** and **stylist** index

photographers

food photographer and stylist index

pages 137 and 139

debbieelder
480 South Peppertree Drive
Gilbert, Arizona 85296
480-551-9769
elderwoodbiz@msn.com

pages 141 and 143

davidlenweaver
510 Hillsdale Avenue
Syracuse, New York 13206
315-463-6908
dave@foodweb.com
www.foodweb.com

pages 165 and 167

marysutkus
420 Limedale Lane
Florissant, Missouri 63031
314-838-5234
mksutkus@aol.com

bibliography

lidiabastianich

Braised Lamb Shanks in Squazet and Tomato and Bread Soup originally appeared in *Lidia's Italian Table* © 1998 William Morrow.

Roasted Pears and Grapes originally appeared in *Lidia's American Kitchen* © 2001 Alfred A. Knopf.

rickbayless

Tortilla Soup with Pasilla Chile, Fresh Cheese and Avocado; Roasted Poblano Guacamole with Garlic and Parsley; Quick-Fried Shrimp with Sweet Toasty Garlic; and Tequila-Flamed Mangoes originally appeared in *Mexico One Plate at a Time* © 2000 Scribner.

tomdouglas

Sweet Goat Cheese Turnovers with Honey, Pistachios and Mint originally appeared in *Tom's Big Dinners* © 2003 Tom Douglas and Jackie Cross.

susanfeniger & marysuemilliken

Basic Red Snapper Ceviche originally appeared in *Mexican Cooking for Dummies* © 1999 For Dummies.

Shrimp and Ancho in a Bath of Garlic originally appeared in *Mesa Mexicana* © 1994 Morrow Cookbooks.

Tomatillo Guacamole and Vanilla Flan originally appeared in *Cooking with Too Hot Tamales* © 1997 Morrow Cookbooks.

galegand & ricktramonto

Frog Leg Risotto with Parsley and Lots of Garlic and Fromage Blanc Mousse originally appeared in *Tru: A Cookbook from the Legendary Chicago Restaurant* © 2004 Random House.

jeniferlang

Mimi's Sauerkraut Cooked with Apples and Boppa's Giblet Gravy originally appeared in *Christmas Memories with Recipes* © 1988 Farrar Straus Giroux.

norapouillon

Sake-Glazed Wild Salmon with Miso Yuzu Vinaigrette and Belgian Endive, Mâche, Beet and Apple Salad with Walnuts and Sherry Vinaigrette originally appeared in *Cooking with Nora* © 1996 Nora Pouillon.

christopherprosperi

The passages by Courtney Febbroriello on pages 112 and 116 originally appeared in *Wife of the Chef: The True Story of a Restaurant and Romance* © 2003 Clarkson Potter.

charlesramseyer

Cumin-Rubbed Sturgeon with Heirloom Tomato Vinaigrette and Black Lentil Chanterelle Ragout and Pacific Oysters on a Spoon originally appeared in *Ray's Boathouse: Seafood Secrets of the Pacific Northwest* © 2003 Documentary Media and Ray's Boathouse.

allensusser

Mango and Crab Salad originally appeared in *The Great Mango Book* © 2001 Ten Speed Press.

charlietrotter

Lobster with Hokkaido Squash Soup and Brown Butter; Serrano Ham and Phyllo-Wrapped Salsify with Bosc Pear and Caramelized Endive; and Bison with Root Vegetable Pavé and Parsnip Purée originally appeared in *The Kitchen Session with Charlie Trotter* © 2004 Ten Speed Press.

recipe index